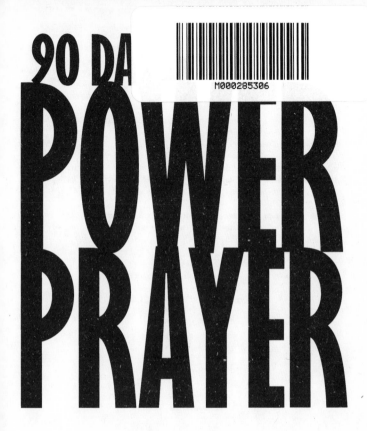

90 DAYS OF POWER PRAYER

KYNAN BRIDGES

WHITAKER HOUSE

Unless otherwise indicated, all Scripture quotations are taken from the King James Version of the Holy Bible. Scripture quotations marked (AMP) are taken from are taken from *The Amplified® Bible*, © 1954, 1958, 1962, 1964, 1965, 1987, 2015 by The Lockman Foundation. Used by permission. (www.Lockman.org). Scripture quotations marked (NKJV) are taken from the *New King James Version*, © 1979, 1980, 1982, 1984 by Thomas Nelson, Inc. Used by permission. All rights reserved.

Boldface type in the Scripture quotations indicates the author's emphasis.

All definitions of Greek words are taken from the New Testament Greek Lexicon—King James Version, based on Thayer's and Smith's Bible Dictionary, plus others (public domain), www.BibleStudyTools.com. All definitions of Hebrew words are taken from the Old Testament Hebrew Lexicon—King James Version, which is the Brown, Driver, Briggs, Gesenius Lexicon (public domain), www.BibleStudyTools.com.

Unless otherwise indicated, dictionary definitions are taken from *Merriam-Webster.com*, 2015, http://www.merriam-webster.com. Definition marked Oxford University Press is taken from *OxfordDictionaries.com*, Oxford University Press, © 2015.

90 Days of Power Prayer:
Supernatural Declarations to Transform Your Life

Kynan Bridges Ministries, Inc.
P.O. Box 159
Ruskin, FL 33575
www.kynanbridges.com
info@kynanbridges.com

ISBN: 978-1-62911-693-8
eBook ISBN: 978-1-62911-694-5
Printed in the United States of America
© 2016 by Kynan Bridges

Whitaker House
1030 Hunt Valley Circle
New Kensington, PA 15068
www.whitakerhouse.com

Library of Congress Cataloging-in-Publication Data (Pending)

3 4 5 6 7 8 9 10 11 **UJ** 23 22 21 20 19 18 17 16

Contents

Preface.. 7

    Day 1: Open Your Eyes 8

    Day 2: Exceeding Abundantly.................................. 11

    Day 3: Soul Prosperity... 14

    Day 4: Financial Breakthrough 17

    Day 5: Breaking Curses 20

    Day 6: Releasing Prophetic Power........................... 23

    Day 7: Divine Healing... 26

    Day 8: The Sound of the Abundance of Rain 29

    Day 9: The Breaker Anointing 32

Day 10: Speak Those Things 35

Day 11: Hearing the Holy Spirit................................. 38

Day 12: Mind Renewal.. 41

Day 13: Prayers of Protection..................................... 44

Day 14: Overcoming the Slumbering Spirit.............. 47

Day 15: Divine Recovery... 50

Day 16: No More Fear.. 53

Day 17: Unlocking the Heavens.................................. 56

Day 18: Your Harvest Is Here!.................................... 58

Day 19: Binding *and* Loosing.................................... 61

Day 20: The Power of Proclamation............................64

Day 21: Too Blessed to Be Stressed........................... 67

Day 22: The Spirit of Intercession 70

Day 23: Deliverance Prayers 73

Day 24: Greater Is He!... 76

Day 25: Good Versus Evil.. 79

Day 26: Don't Stop!..82

Day 27: Destiny Acceleration 84

Day 28: The Spirit of Python 87

Day 29: The Blood of the Lamb 90

Day 30: Supernatural Breakthrough 93

Day 31: The Hearing of Faith..............................96

Day 32: Marriage and Relationships 99

Day 33: The Mind of Christ 102

Day 34: Positive Attitude 105

Day 35: Freedom from Depression 108

Day 36: Purpose and Direction..........................111

Day 37: The Joy of the Lord 113

Day 38: Holiness and Consecration 116

Day 39: Supernatural Favor...............................119

Day 40: Divine Wisdom.....................................122

Day 41: Total Turnaround..................................124

Day 42: All Things Working for Good 127

Day 43: Seeing the Unseen 129

Day 44: Divine Revelation 132

Day 45: More than Conquerors 135

Day 46: Will You Be Made Whole? 137

Day 47: Blessed and Broken................................140

Day 48: The Power of Forgiveness 143

Day 49: Free Indeed!...146

Day 50: No Weapon Formed 148

Day 51: The Tongue of the Learned 151

Day 52: Know the Truth.....................................153

Day 53: Dispelling the Darkness 155

Day 54: Spiritual Awakening 158

Day 55: Developing Spiritual Hunger.............................. 160
Day 56: Lessons from Lazarus 162
Day 57: Purify My Heart.. 165
Day 58: Activate the Grace!... 167
Day 59: Prayers of Vindication 170
Day 60: Confusing the Enemy's Counsel 173
Day 61: Beauty for Ashes.. 175
Day 62: The Aaronic Blessing.. 177
Day 63: Divine Downloads 180
Day 64: The Spirit of Reconciliation 182
Day 65: The Spirit of Prophecy 185
Day 66: Atmospheric Shift 188
Day 67: Your Whole House Shall Be Saved 191
Day 68: Live and Not Die! 193
Day 69: Make Room for Your Miracle 195
Day 70: All Things Are Possible 198
Day 71: The Glory of God 201
Day 72: Just Believe!... 203
Day 73: Don't Look Back 205
Day 74: Arise and Shine.. 208
Day 75: Light Up the Darkness..................................... 210
Day 76: Gideon's Army 213
Day 77: Casting Down Imaginations 216
Day 78: Walking in Love... 219
Day 79: Prayers for Family.. 222
Day 80: Release the Supernatural................................. 225
Day 81: Spiritual Warfare.. 228
Day 82: Piercing the Darkness 231
Day 83: The Children's Bread.. 233

Day 84: The Law of Confession...236
Day 85: Speak to My Heart..239
Day 86: No Turning Back...242
Day 87: Strength in the Inner Man 244
Day 88: Rivers of Living Water..247
Day 89: Overcoming Hopelessness................................250
Day 90: Be of Good Courage..252
About the Author..255

Preface

I can speak from personal experience that few things have been more vital to my walk with the Lord than the spiritual discipline of getting on my knees before Him every morning. The Lord has taught me the hard way that the best way to cement excellent Christian practices in one's life is to repeat them day, by day, by day, building habits that have not just a lifelong impact, but an eternal one! To this end, I have crafted a devotional that I pray will aid you in both understanding and practicing our privilege and responsibility as believers—prophetic prayer.

I challenge you to take this devotional seriously. What I mean by that is to really commit to cracking its cover every day for ninety days. Clear some space in your calendar if you need to, so that you have a few moments every day that are already set aside.

Then, *meditate on the short Scripture* that begins each day. My words are just that—Kynan Bridges' words. But the Scripture is the Holy Word of the all-powerful God who loves us and reigns in us. It is our life! We ignore it at our own risk. Then, *read the devotional* and *pray the prayer out loud* if possible. The devil runs from our prophetic prayers, but the Spirit comes to dwell within them. That is why they are prayers of such power.

I am confident that your life will be transformed by the diligent practice of praying prophetically. In fact, consider this a warning! Pray these prayers—and *don't be surprised if everything changes.*

Day 1: Open Your Eyes

*And it came to pass, as he sat at meat with them, he took bread, and blessed it, and brake, and gave to them. **And their eyes were opened, and they knew him;** and he vanished out of their sight.* (Luke 24:30–31)

One of my favorite childhood games was hide-and-go-seek. I'm sure you all played it, too—or at least some variation of it. The game involves closing your eyes and counting to a certain number while your friends run and hide. Once you finish counting, you are supposed to shout, "Ready or not, here I come!" and start looking. If your friends are really, really good, they can hide from you in plain sight! But when they crawl out from under the couch or slip out of a closet to dash toward base, your eyes are opened—and you know exactly where they are.

Well, that's a little like what the disciples experienced when Jesus opened their eyes to see Him for who He really was. (See Luke 24.) Prior to this experience, the disciples had a limited perspective. They saw Him as the Teacher, the Prophet, and the Rabbi—but not the Son of God. In essence, Christ was hidden from them in plain sight! But after their eyes were opened, they were illuminated to the truth of His heavenly identity. Shortly after this experience, Jesus vanished out of their sight (natural sight that is!), but the revelation of who He was remained. Now the disciples could see Him even more clearly in His absence than when He was physically present. They knew exactly *who* and *where* He was.

The word *"opened"* here comes from the Greek word *dianoigō*, which means "to open one's soul, i.e., to arouse...understanding." In that moment, the disciples received supernatural understanding. Many of us need a similar revelation of who Jesus really is. This spiritual sight must go beyond our religious experiences to a deeper and more profound revelation. God desires to open our eyes in the spiritual realm so that we will be able to understand and comprehend the will and purpose of God for our lives. Paul prayed in Ephesians 1:18, *"The **eyes of your understanding** being enlightened; that ye may know what is the hope of his calling, and what the riches of the glory of his inheritance in the saints."* What would happen if our loved ones received a revelation of the risen Christ, that He alone can forgive our sins and bring eternal life? What would happen if *we* did? Once we and the people we love *open our eyes* to the truth of the risen Christ, we will experience the supernatural power of God in our lives.

9

Day 1: Power Prayer

Father, in the name of Your Son, Jesus Christ, I thank You for who You are and all that You have done in my life. Thank You for opening my spiritual eyes to see the reality of Jesus in my life. I declare that my loved ones are illuminated by Your truth and transformed by the power of Your love. I declare that I walk in supernatural understanding and enlightenment in every area of my life. All spiritual blindness, darkness, and confusion must leave my life right now in Jesus' name! Your Word is a *"lamp unto my feet, and a **light** unto my path"* (Psalm 119:105); therefore, I declare that the Word of God enlightens my decisions, my thinking, my family, and my finances. Every area in my life is blessed because of the light of Your Word shining in and through it. My future and destiny are brighter because of Your truth. I declare that I will no longer yield to deception, falsehood, or wickedness in any area of my life. Jesus, I declare that You are the Lord of my life. I long to follow You and be Your disciple. I declare that, from this day forward, I will see You in the way the Word of God reveals You. My mind is opened and my soul is aroused to the revelation of Jesus Christ. Amen!

10

Day 2: Exceeding Abundantly

*Now unto him that is able to do **exceeding abundantly** above all that we ask or think, according to the power that worketh in us, unto him be glory in the church by Christ Jesus throughout all ages, world without end. Amen.*

(Ephesians 3:20–21)

In John 10:10, Jesus said, *"The thief cometh not, but for to steal, and to kill, and to destroy: I am come that they might have life, and that they might have it more abundantly."* This sounds good, but what does the abundant life look like? First of all, let's look at these two interesting words: *"life"* and *"abundantly."* The word *"life"* comes from the Greek word *zōē*, which means "the absolute fullness of life." The word for *"abundantly"* used in this biblical account is the Greek word *perissos*, which means "over and above, more than is necessary, superadded." Simply put, God wants us to enjoy eternal life (supernatural life) over and above, more than necessary, and exceeding normal measure. That sounds really good!

The problem is that most people relegate eternal life to some future experience, when in fact believers are called to enjoy a supernatural life *here* and *now*. You don't have to wait until you die to experience eternal life. God doesn't desire for us to barely get along while we wait for the "sweet by and by."

The question is, how do we enjoy this abundant life? Paul, in his epistle to the Ephesians, wrote, *"Now unto him that is able to* do **exceeding abundantly** *above all that we ask or think, according to the power that worketh in us.*" The phrase "*exceeding abundantly*" is the same term Jesus used to describe the life He came to give us. In other words, God desires for us to live above circumstances, pain, fear, sickness, rejection, and any other limitations presented to us in the natural realm. He wants us to experience an overcoming life, a life of true victory. The key is found in this phrase, "*according to the power that worketh in us.*" If we want to enjoy the abundant life, we must place a demand on it by faith according to the power of the Spirit that is working in us. The greater the demand, the greater the supply!

Day 2: Power Prayer

Father, in the name of Jesus Christ, I thank You for Your amazing love toward me. Lord, I realize that it is Your will for me to live the abundant life for which Jesus died to give me. I recognize that the enemy has come to steal, kill, and destroy, but You have come to impart Your eternal life to me, here and now! I don't have to wait to enjoy the benefits of eternity, because You have called me to walk in the supernatural every day. I declare that Your supernatural power is at work inside of me. You are able to do exceeding abundantly in my life through the power of Your Word operating in my inner being. I declare that sickness, poverty, disease, and oppression are broken by the power of the Holy Spirit working in me. I will never live beneath the abundant life that You have provided for me. I am no longer limited by my circumstances or problems, but I operate in the unlimited power of God's Word. I live a victorious life, and there are no forces in heaven or in earth greater than the Holy Spirit living in me. I will never be depressed! I will never be afraid! I will never be bound again! I declare that the same Spirit that raised Jesus from the dead lives in me, and quickens every area of my life in Jesus' name! Amen.

Day 3: Soul Prosperity

Beloved, I wish above all things that thou mayest prosper and be in health, even as thy soul prospereth.

(3 John 2:2)

When the psalmist prayed for his beloved city of Jerusalem, a city that symbolized the presence of God with the Israelites, he prayed specifically for peace: *"Pray for the peace of Jerusalem"* (Psalm 122:6). Why peace? We might immediately think of peace from conflict or a ceasefire, and that is certainly true. However, the Hebrew word for peace packs more than the English term: *"peace"* in Hebrew is *shalom*, which means wholeness, completeness, and prosperity. *Shalom* is an all-encompassing term for well-being and restoration on every level.

It is God's will that you and I, too, have *shalom*, that we prosper in every area in our lives. The most important form of prosperity is the prosperity that takes place in our soul. This is what the apostle John was alluding to in his third epistle when he writes this wish that his readers will prosper even as their souls prosper. The Greek word used here for *"prosper"* is *euodoō*, which means "to grant a prosperous and expeditious journey, to lead by a direct and easy way." God wants us to have everything that we need in order to do everything that He has called us to do. Imagine a farmer that doesn't possess plowing equipment or a painter without a paintbrush. They wouldn't get much done! In a similar way, we need *shalom* to be able to get anything done!

God doesn't want us to be lacking in any area of our lives, especially our souls. This means that God wants us to have *shalom* in our mind, decisions, and emotions. The more peace we have in our soul, the more we will experience outward success and abundance in our lives. Remember, prosperity is from the inside out and not the outside in! *Shalom* to you in Jesus' name!

Day 3: Power Prayer

Father, in the name of Jesus, I thank You for Your peace and prosperity in every area of my life. Jesus, I know that You are the Prince of Peace; therefore, I declare that Your supernatural peace floods my soul. I command all fear, chaos, confusion, and despair to leave me now. I declare that I am complete and whole in every area of my life. I have been justified by faith through the Lord Jesus Christ; therefore, I have peace with God. I declare that anything that is contrary to peace in my life is neutralized in Jesus' name. I declare that I walk in divine prosperity. I have an abundance of peace, resources, and blessings. There is nothing missing and nothing broken in any area of my life because of Jesus. I am no longer a slave to chaos and confusion. Circumstances no longer determine my level of peace within, because I am prosperous on the inside. I have a victorious and productive mental attitude. All negativity and cynicism must leave my thought life right now. You said You would keep me in perfect peace if my mind was stayed on You; therefore, I declare that I have perfect peace and I walk in biblical prosperity. There is no lack or insufficiency in any area of my life. Your Word declares that You give me richly all things to enjoy, therefore I rejoice in Your goodness and abundant provision in my life. In Jesus' name, amen!

16

Believing in The worst of people, HAVE A HARD Time Seeing The good in anyone

Day 4: Financial Breakthrough

*And he commanded the multitude to sit down on the grass,
and took the five loaves, and the two fishes, and looking up
to heaven, he blessed, and brake, and gave the loaves to his
disciples, and the disciples to the multitude.*

(Matthew 14:19)

Many years ago, I was in a state of financial lack. It was so bad that there were even times when I didn't know where my next meal was going to come from. Ironically, I loved the Lord and was aware of many Scriptures on financial abundance—at least, so I thought! However, I was taught that prosperity was an ungodly thing. I was under the impression that it wasn't truly the will of God for me to prosper. Then, one day, I read a verse in the Bible that literally transformed my life: "*And God is able to make all grace abound toward you; that ye, **always having all sufficiency in all things**, may abound to every good work*" (2 Corinthians 9:8). In the *Amplified Bible*, it is even more descriptive: "*And God is able to make all grace [every favor and earthly blessing] come in abundance to you, so that you may always [under all circumstances, regardless of the need] have complete sufficiency in everything [being completely self-sufficient in Him], and have an abundance for every good work and act of charity.*"

This sure didn't look like the kind of life I was experiencing at the time! Simply put, I was in need of a supernatural financial breakthrough in my life. Remember, without revelation there can be no transformation. Even though I read a few Scriptures, I didn't have a revelation of God's will for my finances, and faith can only operate where the will of God is known. God wanted me to walk in financial abundance. He wanted me to experience supernatural multiplication in my life. In the Gospel accounts, Jesus took two fish and five loaves of bread and multiplied them. (See Matthew 14:19.) God has the ability to take the little that we have and use it to feed multitudes as long as we are willing to trust it in His hands. What if I told you that the breakthrough you were looking for was already in your hands? Release the little that is in your hands, and God will release the abundance that is in His!

Day 4: Power Prayer

Father, in the name of Jesus, I thank You for Your miraculous provision in my life. I declare breakthrough in every area of my financial life. Every Jericho wall surrounding my blessings, prosperity, and finances comes down right now in Jesus' name! All contracts, deals, judgments, opportunities, and lands are released to me right now in Jesus' name. No weapon fashioned against me or my resources will prosper, and I take authority over every devouring spirit that has robbed or hindered the blessings of God from flowing into my life. My mind and spirit are receptive to supernatural opportunities, divine ideas, and witty inventions in the name of Jesus. According to Deuteronomy 8:18, I receive power and ability to get wealth so that Your covenant may be established and Your kingdom advanced in the earth. I live in the reality of Your prosperous plan for my life. Today, I declare that my financial breakthrough has come in Jesus' name. Amen!

Day 5: Breaking Curses

Christ hath redeemed us from the curse of the law, being made a curse for us: for it is written, Cursed is every one that hangeth on a tree: that the blessing of Abraham might come on the Gentiles through Jesus Christ; that we might receive the promise of the Spirit through faith.

(Galatians 3:13–14)

Sticks and stones may break my bones, but words can never hurt me!" I'm sure, like me, you chanted this little adage on the playground, maybe to prompt self-esteem or bravery. Well, as nice as this phrase is, it couldn't be further from the truth: Words have tremendous power! Words can hurt and they can heal. Words can invoke blessings or they can invoke curses. As a child, I thought that curses were the result of witches brewing toad feet in a cauldron (thanks to Disney cartoons). Little did I know, back then, that curses were much more subtle, and much more destructive. A curse is defined as a solemn utterance intended to invoke a supernatural power to inflict harm or punishment on someone or something. Every time someone speaks evil over another person, they are, in effect, cursing them. This is why the Scriptures command us to *"bless, and curse not"* (Romans 12:14).

In the Old Testament, God said that He would visit the iniquities of the fathers upon the children, to the third and fourth generation. (See Exodus 34:6–7.) This was another dimension

20

of a curse. Iniquitous patterns can be perpetuated through bloodlines (and also as a result of solemn utterances), giving legal permission to demonic spirits to oppress individuals, families, children, and even communities—often for generations. Before we became born again, we lived under a curse. This curse of sin, sickness, poverty, and, ultimately, death affected every area of our lives.

I have good news for you; through Christ, the curse has been broken off of our lives! Christ became a curse for us so that we no longer have to live under the influence of curses; rather, we have been liberated and empowered to walk in the fullness of the blessing! The key to walking in the blessing is coming into agreement with the blessing and falling out of agreement with the curse. Whatever you agree with is what you give legal permission to operate in your life. Whom God blesses, no man can curse.

Day 5: Power Prayer

Father, in the name of Jesus Christ, I take authority over the spirits of darkness, depression, death, and destruction in the name of Jesus. I now invoke my heavenly rights as a citizen of the kingdom of God, and declare that through the shed blood of Jesus, I am healed, whole, and delivered. I decree that all curses and strongholds are broken off my life and the lives of those I love. I take authority over the spirit of death (premature or otherwise) *right now*. I declare that no weapon formed against Your people will prosper. I let loose the love, joy, peace, wholeness, and protection of God *now*! Send your angels to encamp all around me. I declare that the very *power and presence* of God fills my being from the crown of my head to the soles of my feet. I declare that all spiritual leaders and laborers are covered in the blood of Jesus Christ. I command schizophrenia, hypocrisy, double-mindedness, confusion, depression, despair, loneliness, bipolar disorder, and any other mental stronghold or mind-binding spirit to lose its power and to loosen its hold on the people of God right now, in Jesus' name. The joy of the Lord is my strength! From this day forward, I walk in total and complete freedom and victory. In Jesus' name, amen!

22

Day 6: Releasing Prophetic Power

Thou shalt also decree a thing, and it shall be established unto thee: and the light shall shine upon thy ways.

(Job 22:28)

One of the most profound yet underestimated realities in the body of Christ is the power of our words. In fact, as born-again believers, our words are pregnant with supernatural power. What if I told you that whatever you said would come to pass? Would you continue to say the same things that you are saying now? The Scripture tells us plainly, *"Death and life are in **the power of the tongue**: and they that love it shall eat the fruit thereof"* (Proverbs 18:21). The word *"power"* in this verse is derived from the Hebrew word *yad*, which is translated "hand." In other words, the power of life and death are in the hands (or strength) of your tongue. Your tongue is a divine mechanism for releasing prophetic power.

If you were constructing a building, the integrity and soundness of that building would be determined by how efficiently you used your hands. In the same way, the quality of our lives will be determined by how biblically sound we are with our tongue and our words. The Bible says, *"Thou shalt also decree a thing and it shall be established."* The *Amplified Bible* puts it this way: *"You will also decide and decree a thing, and it will be established for you; and the light [of God's favor] will shine upon your ways."* The key to experiencing favor, blessing, increase, and prosperity in your life is in your mouth. Most people think of prophecy as something ominous and exclusive to people who hold titles in the church, but the truth is that all of us have been given the power and responsibility both to prophesy to the situations and circumstances of our lives and to decree God's Word. When we decree the Word of God, we release the favor and prophetic promises of God into our lives. I don't know about you, but I am excited about God's favor!

Day 6: Power Prayer

Father, in Jesus' name, I declare that Your Word is packed with miraculous power. You said that if I decree a thing, it would be established unto me; therefore, I declare that Your goodness, mercy, favor, and supernatural help abound in my life. I speak crop failure to every tree that is not bringing forth good fruit. I declare that it is well with my mind, emotions, finances, relationships, health, and ministry in the name of Jesus. Everything that You have promised to me will be made manifest in my life in due season. I declare that any and all stagnation, delay, blockage, or demonic interference is broken, in Jesus' name, and the spiritual airways are cleared to receive the blessings and divine assistance that have been assigned to my life. I prophesy to every area of barrenness in my life or the lives of those I am praying for, and I say, "flourish!" I declare that nothing shall separate me from the plan and purpose of God for my life. My days are becoming greater and my future is becoming brighter as I place my faith and confidence in the Word of God. Your Word is a lamp unto my feet and a light unto my path. I am blessed, restored, and delivered in Jesus' name! Amen.

Day 7: Divine Healing

Who his own self bare our sins in his own body on the tree, that we, being dead to sins, should live unto righteousness: **by whose stripes ye were healed.**   (1 Peter 2:24)

Whether you realize it or not, healing is the children's bread. Healing is the divine inheritance of every believer. Contrary to what many people believe, healing is not just something that God will do if it is His will. Healing *belongs* to us! David said, *"I have been young, and now am old; yet have I not seen the righteous forsaken, nor his* **seed begging bread**" (Psalm 37:25). In other words, God as a loving Father will not neglect His children.

Jesus put it this way, *"For every one that asketh receiveth; and he that seeketh findeth; and to him that knocketh it shall be opened. Or what man is there of you, whom if his son ask bread, will he give him a stone? Or if he ask a fish, will he give him a serpent? If ye then, being evil, know how to give good gifts unto your children, how much more shall your Father which is in heaven give good things to them that ask him?"* (Matthew 7:8–11). If natural parents would not do anything to harm their children, then why would we think that putting sickness and disease on His children somehow pleases God? The devil would have us believe that, but he is a clever liar!

Jesus paid a tremendous price for our healing. By His stripes we were healed from every category of sickness, disease, and infirmity, from the common cold to cancer. I don't know about you, but I refuse to "take on" something that Jesus died to "take off" of my life. Jesus instructed His disciples to ask for their daily bread. (See Matthew 6:11.) Healing is the daily bread of the believer, and through the blood of Jesus we have received a never-ending supply of God's miraculous healing power. Whatever illness, ailment, infirmity, or symptom you or your loved ones might be dealing with, you must understand that Jesus addressed it on the cross. You are already healed, completely and totally!

Day 7: Power Prayer

Father, in the name of Jesus, I thank You that, because of Christ's blood, I am completely and totally healed of any and all sicknesses and infirmities. Thank You, Father, that I am healed completely through the atoning work of Jesus Christ on the cross. Every cell in my body must submit to the lordship of Jesus Christ. Every part of my body functions perfectly. Every fiber of my being is under the control and authority of the Word of God. I am healed and whole in the name of Jesus. According to 1 Peter 2:24, the stripes of Jesus have categorically healed me from all disease; therefore, sickness has no more legal right to operate in my life. I serve the enemy notice that the debt of sin and iniquity has been satisfied on the cross. The penalty of my sin has been paid in full, and I no longer have any outstanding debt. I am free to walk in divine health and fulfill my assignment in wholeness and completeness. I command all lying symptoms to cease and desist in the name of Jesus. Cancer, autoimmune disorders, hypertension, diabetes, issues of blood, arthritis, depression, and any other disease; I command you to leave my body in the name of Jesus. I am healed! Amen!

Day 8: The Sound of the Abundance of Rain

And Elijah said unto Ahab, Get thee up, eat and drink;
for there is a sound of abundance of rain.

(1 Kings 18:41)

O ne of my favorite prophets in the Old Testament was the prophet Elijah, perhaps because of the incredible showdown we learn of in 1 Kings 18 when Elijah singlehandedly defeated and killed the prophets of Baal and lifted the spiritual and actual drought that hovered over the land of ancient Israel. After three and a half years of not even a single raindrop, the prophet confidently declared, "I hear the sound of the abundance of rain."

You may not feel like an Elijah right now, but I believe that God is about to manifest His abundant rain in your life. Do you hear the sound? Remember, Elijah heard the rain long before he even saw the rain. After Elijah heard the rain, seven times, as he was praying for rain on top of Mount Carmel, he asked his servant to look for an oncoming cloud. It was only after the seventh time that his servant finally saw something and said, *"Behold, there ariseth a little cloud out of the sea, like a man's hand"* (1 Kings 18:44).

From this we clearly learn that the spiritual realm operates by sound and not by sight. The Bible says, *"For we walk by faith, not by sight"* (2 Corinthians 5:7). The Bible goes further to say,

*"So then **faith cometh by hearing**, and hearing by the word of God"* (Romans 10:17). In other words, our faith is determined by the sound we are hearing. Elijah heard a sound that completely contradicted what he saw in the natural realm, yet his ears were in tune with God.

Are you willing to hear the sound of your healing, breakthrough, and deliverance? Too many people are looking at what they see, but they are not hearing the promises of God! I have learned over the years that looks can be deceiving. Every blessing and miracle that God has manifested in my life came as a result of a supernatural sound that preceded its manifestation in the natural. Open your spiritual ears and hear the sound of the abundance of rain! The rain is already here!

Day 8: Power Prayer

Father, in the name of Jesus, I thank You for Your abundant prophetic promises in my life. Your Word declares that faith comes by hearing and hearing by the Word of God; therefore, I declare that my spiritual ears are opened and receptive to Your Word. By faith I hear the sound of the abundance of rain. I declare that a supernatural harvest of blessings, favor, and prosperity abound to my heavenly account. All drought, lack, and insufficiency are lifted from my life, spiritually and naturally. I am not moved by what I see. I am not moved by the report of men. I am moved by the Word of God alone. Thank You, Father, for the power of Your Word in my life! No matter what the enemy presents to me, I choose to make the Word of God the very final authority in my life. I hear the sound of breakthrough, healing, deliverance raining on my life in Jesus' name. I walk under an open heaven in every area of my life. I declare that the rain is here and the heavens are opened. I don't have to wait to see any blessings manifest, because I know by faith that I am already blessed with all spiritual blessings in heavenly places in Christ. Thank You for Your goodness and favor in my life. I declare that everything is turning around for my good in Jesus' name! Amen.

Day 9: The Breaker Anointing

*I will surely assemble, O Jacob, all of thee; I will surely gather the remnant of Israel....The **breaker** is come up before them: they have broken up, and have passed through the gate, and are gone out by it: and their king shall pass before them, and the LORD on the head of them.*

(Micah 2:12–13)

Jesus was anointed by God to heal the sick, cast out demons, and set the oppressed free. This was the key to unlocking His earthly ministry. We can learn this from His own words: *"The Spirit of the Lord is upon me, because he hath anointed me to preach the gospel to the poor; he hath sent me to heal the brokenhearted, to preach deliverance to the captives, and recovering of sight to the blind, to set at liberty them that are bruised, to preach the acceptable year of the Lord"* (Luke 4:18–19).

Acts 10:38 tells us, *"God anointed Jesus of Nazareth with the Holy Ghost and with power: who went about doing good, and healing all that were oppressed of the devil; for God was with him."* We know that Jesus is God, but we also know that He was the Son of Man, anointed with the power of God. In other words, it was the anointing of the Holy Spirit in and upon Jesus that destroyed yokes of bondage. Jesus came to fulfill messianic prophecy as stated in Isaiah 61. This same anointing is available to every single born-again believer today. Just like the people during the Bible days needed to experience a powerful anointing in order to shift their lives and circumstances, you and I also need to experience this same anointing.

In the book of Micah, the children of Israel were bound, and the prophet Micah prophesied, *"The breaker is come up before them."* "Breaker" is the Hebrew word *parats*, which means "breakthrough." This is what I call the breaker anointing. The breaker anointing is the yoke-destroying, burden-removing power of God, which causes us to experience supernatural breakthrough in our lives. In other words, this anointing has the power to break barriers, patterns, and life-controlling issues that are operating in our lives or in the lives of those we are praying for. It doesn't matter how long you have been bound or how difficult the situation, the breaker anointing is more powerful than any obstacle that stands before you.

33

Day 9: Power Prayer

Father, in the name of Jesus, I thank You for the anointing that You have placed upon my life. Thank You, Lord, that You have released the yoke-destroying and burden-removing anointing that produces supernatural breakthrough in every area of my life. Thank You, Lord, that this breaker anointing is being released right now. I declare that any and all bondage—stagnation, hindrances, or resistance in my life—is broken by the power of the Holy Spirit. Every blessing and promise held captive by the enemy must be released right now in Jesus' name. I declare that the Anointed One (Jesus Christ) and His anointing is activated and released in my life. I thank You, Lord, that all demonic activity is seized and the angels of God are loosed to war on my behalf in Jesus' name. By faith, I break out of any and all forms of captivity. Your Word says that I will know the truth and the truth will make me free; therefore, I declare that I am made free by the blood of the Lamb and by the Word of my testimony. Thank You, Lord, for total freedom and victory in my life in Jesus' name. Amen!

34

Day 10: Speak Those Things

*(As it is written, I have made thee a father of many nations,) before him whom he believed, even God, who quickeneth the dead, and calleth those things which be not **as though they were**.*
(Romans 4:17)

I grew up at the younger end of a large family. With so many older siblings, I quickly learned how to use words to my own advantage—including threatening others when I felt intimidated, being quick to talk back when bullied or criticized, and a plethora of other verbal skills necessary for survival. I thought, back then, that I could manipulate a situation by my words. I've since learned something far more profound, and far more positive: we can *create* a situation by our words. We literally have the ability to speak things, situations, and circumstances into existence.

This spiritual principle has been hijacked by the New Age community, but make no mistake, it is absolutely biblical! For example, have you ever said that you feel a certain way—that you're sick, upset, frustrated, or depressed? What happens when you speak those words? Immediately, the feeling that you articulated takes root in your mind and emotions, and even your physical body. This is a very powerful phenomenon! Scientists have concluded that words affect our behavior in a very tangible way.

What would happen if you and I would learn to speak God's Word over our lives instead of words of doom and gloom?

I believe that we would experience a supernatural mega-thrust into our lives. Jesus said in Mark 11:22–23, *"And Jesus answering saith unto them,* **Have faith in God***. For verily I say unto you, that whosoever shall say unto this mountain, Be thou removed, and be thou cast into the sea; and shall not doubt in his heart, but shall believe that those things which he saith shall come to pass; he shall have whatsoever he saith."* Notice that the Bible never told us to *say* what we *have*, it said that we would *have* what we *say*! When he was promised an heir, Abraham did not consider his own impotence nor the barrenness of Sarah's womb, but he believed he would be the "*father of many nations*" (Genesis 17:4) despite any physical evidence to the contrary. You and I must learn how to call those things that be not as though they were, and thus become imitators of our heavenly Father.

36

Day 10: Power Prayer

Father, in the name of Jesus, I recognize that You are the most powerful Being in all the universe. Your Word has the ability to create and to give life. Just as You spoke the world into existence through Your living Word, I speak that same Word over every barren area in my life. In the beginning was the Word, and the Word was with God, and the Word was God (see John 1:1); therefore, I declare that Your Word is the final authority in my life. I make the decision by faith to declare Your Word despite what I see, hear, or feel in the natural world. I recognize that real faith is not the ignorance or neglect of circumstances but dominion over them. Your Word is alive, active, and full of supernatural power. I release that supernatural power now by declaring Your Word. I will not die, but live and declare the works of the Lord. (See Psalm 118:17.) My life is productive, fruitful, and blessed in every area. No weapon fashioned against me shall prosper because I am a child of the Most High God and His supernatural grace covers me completely. I am healed, blessed, prospered, and restored in Jesus' name. I can do all things through Christ who gives me strength in Jesus' name. Amen!

37

Day 11: Hearing the Holy Spirit

As the Holy Ghost saith, To day if ye will hear his voice, harden not your hearts, as in the provocation, in the day of temptation in the wilderness: when your fathers tempted me, proved me, and saw my works forty years. Wherefore I was grieved with that generation, and said, They do always err in their heart; and they have not known my ways.

(Hebrews 3:7–10)

During the summer of 1996, I met the most important person on earth. Our encounter changed my life forever. This person was unlike anybody I had ever met before. Words cannot describe the way I felt and the exhilarating rush that went through my entire being when I was in this person's presence; this person was gentle, kind, patient, and infinitely wise.

You are probably thinking that I am talking about my wife, but you would be wrong (although she definitely possesses infinite wisdom). I am speaking of none other than the Holy Spirit. He is the most important Person on earth. Unfortunately, He is also one of the most neglected persons on earth!

Who is the Holy Spirit? I am so glad you asked! Jesus promised in John 15:26, *"But when the **Comforter** is come, whom I will send unto you from the Father, even the Spirit of truth, which proceedeth from the Father, he shall testify of me."* The Holy Spirit is the Spirit of God, the Spirit of Jesus Christ on earth. He is referred to as the *"Comforter"*; the Greek word is *paraklētos*, which means "the one called to our side to plead our cause." Simply put, the Holy Spirit is our divine Helper in the earthly realm. He helps our infirmities. He teaches us how to pray, and He testifies of the risen Christ. He is also the One responsible for manifesting the gifts and power of God in our lives. The question is, how can we receive help from the Helper if we don't hear Him? You and I must develop the discipline of hearing His voice if we want to live a supernatural life. What is the Holy Spirit saying to you today? Do you hear His voice? Today the Holy Spirit desires to speak to you. Harden not your heart!

Day 11: Power Prayer

Father, in the name of Jesus, I thank You for who You are and all that You have done. I declare in the name of Jesus Christ that I have intimacy with the Holy Spirit. I have a personal relationship with You through Your Spirit. I hear the voice of the Holy Spirit on a consistent basis. I receive strategic direction from the Holy Spirit as it relates to my finances, relationships, choices, occupation, calling, witnessing, and every other area in my life. I love to hear the voice of the Spirit. Lord, I thank You for divine clarity in every area of my life. I declare that there is no more confusion in my mind or spirit, because the water of the Word cleanses my soul. Just like a radio is tuned to a station and receives that particular transmission, I am tuned in to heaven's frequency and I receive divine insight, wisdom, and revelation in Jesus' name. I decree that every voice in my life that is not the voice of the Holy Spirit is silenced right now in Jesus' name! Amen.

40

Day 12: Mind Renewal

I beseech you therefore, brethren, by the mercies of God, that ye present your bodies a living sacrifice, holy, acceptable unto God, which is your reasonable service. And be not conformed to this world: but be ye transformed by the renewing of your mind, that ye may prove what is that good, and acceptable, and perfect, will of God.

(Romans 12:1–2)

Our mind is one of the most important components of our Christian experience. The Bible says plainly, *"For as [a man] thinketh in his heart, so is he"* (Proverbs 23:7). I like to rephrase that to, "What you set your mind on, you will ultimately manifest." Many believers love God with all their hearts, but they are unable to manifest the abundant life that Christ gave them, because they have not understood the importance and significance of mind renewal.

What does it mean to renew our minds and why is it so important? In Paul's epistle to the Romans, he instructs us to *"be ye transformed by the renewing of your mind."* The word *"transformed"* comes from the same Greek root word that gives us "metamorphosis." A metamorphosis is a change of the form or nature of a thing or person into a completely different one, by natural or supernatural means. In other words, we are changed in our natural expression through the renewing (renovating) of our mind. Once we became born-again, we became new creations in Christ (see 2 Corinthians 5:17), but we must appropriate this spiritual reality into every sphere of our lives. In essence, we have to "work out" what God has "worked-in." The more we meditate on God's Word, the more we begin to manifest this new life. This is why the things that we meditate on are so vitally important. Many people have what I call "stinking thinking"; that is to say, they are always focused on negativity, defeat, and despair. Let us not be among those who possess a defeated mind-set! Too many believers are losing the battle in their minds. For example, don't say to yourself, "I am just a sinner!" because the reality is that you are the righteousness of God in Christ! The more we think on the Word, the more the Word will transform our lives.

Day 12: Power Prayer

Father, in the name of Jesus, I thank You for Your everlasting goodness toward me. Your Word declares, *"Therefore if any man be in Christ, he is a new creature: old things are passed away; behold, all things are become new"* (2 Corinthians 5:17). I declare that I am a new creation in Christ; old things have passed away, and I have become brand new. I am no longer controlled or manipulated by my past sins, failures, and iniquities, but I have been made clean by the atoning blood of Jesus Christ. By faith I possess the mind of Christ! I submit my thought life to the Word of God and declare that I think and reason like Jesus. I command any and all mind-binding spirits to leave me now in Jesus' name. My heart is receptive to Your truth, and Your Word renews my mind. The more I think on godly things, the more I am changed into the image and character of Jesus Christ. I declare that the life of almighty God is made manifest in and through me daily. I declare that the peace of God that passes all understanding rules my heart and mind in the name of Jesus. Amen!

43

Day 13: Prayers of Protection

He that dwelleth in the secret place of the most High shall abide under the shadow of the Almighty. I will say of the Lord, He is my refuge and my fortress: my God; in him will I trust. Surely he shall deliver thee from the snare of the fowler, and from the noisome pestilence.

(Psalm 91:1–3)

I have come to discover firsthand the reality of divine protection. On one of my mission trips to Liberia, I encountered an extremely perilous situation. I was called upon to preach three times a day for six days straight in a small township outside of Monrovia. It was extremely exhausting, but even worse was what I witnessed during the meetings: people everywhere seemed very sick, and some were even vomiting during the service. I later learned that shortly before I arrived, the Ebola virus had broken out in Liberia.

I had already prayed Psalm 91 over my entire trip, and I had intercessors praying prayers of protection for me back in the States. I declared that no evil would befall my dwelling and that I would be delivered from the *"noisome pestilence."* By the grace of God, I didn't get sick in the slightest. A month after I came back from Liberia, there were reports of thousands of people who had been infected and killed by the deadly Ebola virus. This was wretched and dreadful news! Yet I was in awe and rejoicing that there was no negative impact on me. In addition to this, not a single pastor or parishioner in our ministerial fellowship saw a single fatality from the Ebola outbreak. Glory to God! This is what we call "divine protection." Through prayer, we activated God's promise of protection as outlined in Psalm 91.

Not only do I use this powerful prayer when I travel overseas, but I pray this prayer every day. Every time I travel (by car or plane) I declare, "I dwell in the secret place of the Most High God, and I abide under the shadow of the Almighty. I declare divine protection over every aspect of my journey, in Jesus' name! Amen!" Remember, the Scripture says, *"Ask, and ye shall receive"* (John 16:24). How many areas of our lives could use God's divine protection? We don't have to experience calamity, peril, or chaos in our lives. We have the privilege of dwelling under the shadow of His wings. We can pray this prayer of divine protection over our homes, families, children, churches, schools, neighborhoods, and places of employment. We can dwell in the secret place!

Day 13: Power Prayer

Father, in the name of Jesus, I thank You for Your goodness and grace toward me. Thank You, Lord, for Your divine protection over my life. I declare that I dwell in the secret place of the Most High, and I abide under the shadow of the Almighty. Thank You, God, for being my refuge and safety. I declare that I am covered under the shadow of Your wings and my trust is in Your power and might. I am delivered from every snare of the wicked one and any and all pestilence, virus, disease, infection, or outbreak, in Jesus' name. I declare that no evil (in any form) can come near my dwelling or my family, in Jesus' name. Sickness, disease, and infirmity have no place in my life. Lord, I thank You for dispatching Your angels of protection to go before me and keep me in all of Your ways. I am protected from catastrophe, chaos, accidents, calamity, peril, danger, harm, and destruction in the name of Jesus Christ. I will dwell in peace and safety today, and every day, of my life. A thousand shall fall by my side and ten thousand at my right hand, but destruction will not come near me. I am not afraid of any demonic activity or assignment from the devil, because greater is He who lives in me than he that lives in the world. (See 1 John 4:4.) I am surrounded with a host of warring angels that hearken to the voice of God's Word and who are ready to move at my beckoning call. In Jesus' name, amen.

Day 14: Overcoming the Slumbering Spirit

Wherefore he saith, Awake thou that sleepest, and arise from the dead, and Christ shall give thee light.

(Ephesians 5:14)

Have you ever found it difficult to pray or read the Word of God? Have you ever found yourself feeling apathetic toward the things of God? Has worship seemed a difficult task lately? You might be afflicted by something called a slumbering spirit!

I believe that this is an insidious attempt by the enemy to keep you and me from experiencing the power of God in our lives. I can remember sitting in church and at times feeling an overwhelming sleepiness come over me. The irony is that once the sermon was over or church was released, I would have a sudden jolt of exuberance. Is this a coincidence? Absolutely not! Unfortunately, there are many people who are being affected by a slumbering spirit, and most of them don't even realize it.

There is a medical condition known as sleep paralysis, in which a person is in between a state of sleep and awareness; they are unable to move, speak, or react. Many people believe this to be a demonic manifestation. In the same way, the enemy has attempted to paralyze the church with slumber so that we will not be able to move in our kingdom assignment, or respond to the presence of God. When people are under the influence of a slumbering spirit, they are not awake to the things of God. They are literally in a drunken state of mind and spirit.

It is not natural for believers to be apathetic toward spiritual things. It is not natural for us to see prayer as some difficult task that we can hardly bear. We were created for the presence of God. In fact, we are at our best when we are in His presence. It is time for us to shake off the slumbering spirit, and put on the garment of praise. The season of dullness, apathy, and indifference is over! God wants to commune with His people, and we must be awake and alert in order to hear what the Holy Spirit is speaking to the church. God is sending a wave of revival in the area of prayer, intercession, and worship. It is time for us to desire God more than anything else in our lives.

Day 14: Power Prayer

Right now, in the mighty name of Jesus Christ, and through the power of His omnipotent blood, I declare that the slumbering spirit is broken off of my life and the lives of those I love. I declare that I am awakened to the things of God and that the Holy Spirit invigorates me. I command all slumber, laziness, apathy, indifference, and dullness toward the things of God to leave me right now in Jesus' name. Thank You, Lord, that the fire of Your presence burns within the chambers of my heart. I love Your presence! I love to commune with You in prayer! Thank You, Holy Spirit, for revealing the heart of the Father to me right now! I am activated in my supernatural purpose and destiny. I declare that my zeal, enthusiasm, and charisma are contagious. People want more of God because of me! I declare that I possess a fresh hunger and desire for the things of God. Lord, I thank You for restoring the joy of my salvation. (See Psalm 51:12.) I prophesy to every dry, stagnant, empty, and dead area in my life, and I say "Arise in Jesus' name!" I declare that anything in my life that is choking, smothering, or extinguishing my worship must be removed in the name of Jesus. Amen!

Day 15: Divine Recovery

*And David enquired at the L*ORD*, saying, Shall I pursue after this troop? Shall I overtake them? And he answered him, Pursue: for thou shalt surely overtake them, **and without fail recover all**.* (1 Samuel 30:8)

Oﾠne of the most frustrating things in life, in my opinion, is losing something of value. For example, I am extremely fond of pens. I consider myself an amateur pen collector. On one occasion, I misplaced a pen that was expensive and one of the best in my collection. When I realized that I lost it, I became very upset! I looked everywhere for the pen but after several months of searching, I decided that the pen was permanently lost, and I gave up. Almost a year later, however, I was looking for some documents in the glove compartment of my car, and to my surprise, I found my precious pen. It was in perfect condition! Glory to God!

You may not be a pen collector like me, but there may be other things in your life that you find extremely precious that have been stolen by the enemy of your soul. Maybe it was your peace, your health, your financial security, your family, or a precious relationship. Regardless of what was lost, however, whether big or small, God desires to bring restoration and recovery to your life.

King David of Israel knew all too well the pain of loss. Once, on his return home from attempting to battle his enemy, he found that his city had been pillaged and burned with fire, and, even worse, that the enemy had abducted his family. Instead of giving in to despair, however, David *"encouraged himself in the* LORD*"* (1 Samuel 30:6), and asked the Lord whether or not he should pursue what was lost. God responded, *"Pursue: for thou shalt surely overtake them, and without fail recover all."* This attitude of confidence of the restoration of all that God has promised to us should be reflected in our everyday life! When I found my precious pen, my frustration was turned into rejoicing. God is about to turn your tears into rejoicing. You will recover all! I declare that whatever was lost, stolen, or abducted is about to be recovered in Jesus' name. The key is seeking the Lord with all of your heart. As you seek Him, you will receive an impartation of grace and courage to pursue. Do not give up! This is your season of divine recovery.

Day 15: Power Prayer

Thank You, Lord Jesus, for being my Deliverer and Restorer. Through the cross, You have purchased my freedom and victory. Your blood has redeemed me from destruction, atoned for my sins, and made me whole. I declare that any and every good thing that You have ordained for my life that the enemy has seemed to steal, sabotage, hinder, or delay is restored with interest. I declare that the cankerworm and devourer (see Malachi 3:11) must release all provisions, contracts, and opportunities that God has given me in the name of Jesus. I declare that *all* losses stop right now! In Jesus' name, amen!

Day 16: No More Fear

*For God hath not given us the **spirit of fear**; but of power,*
and of love, and of a sound mind.   (2 Timothy 1:7)

Years ago, I was daily tormented by fear. I can remember being afraid to go to sleep at night because of the nightmares and horrifying spiritual attacks I would experience. It was then that I realized that the kingdom of darkness was very real. I discovered that one of Satan's greatest weapons is fear. Why? Because he knows that you and I will not take authority over something we fear. What is fear? Simply put, fear is timidity or cowardice resulting from a wrong belief system. I also like to define fear as false evidence appearing true! We are told in 2 Timothy that God has not given us a spirit of fear. Wow! This tells us that fear is in fact a spirit, and this spirit does not come from God. God doesn't want us to succumb to the lies of the evil one in the form of fear and ignorance.

Fear comes in many forms. Many people are afraid of failure, others are fearful of being alone, and others still are fearful of death. No matter what fear has attempted to attach itself to your life, you must understand that God has not given you a spirit of fear; instead, He has equipped you with power, love, and a sound mind.

Whenever we are operating in fear, we are neutralizing our spiritual power and authority. Beloved, I don't know about you, but I don't like being afraid! One day, while I was being attacked in my sleep by demonic spirits, I screamed the name of Jesus. Suddenly, the oppression lifted! It was then that I realized that the name of Jesus was stronger than the devil. There is no need to fear the enemy. He has no power in your life except that which you give him. Every fear in our lives is the result of a lie we have believed about God, ourselves, or others; however, the moment we accept God's truth, the power of the lie is broken and fear leaves. The Scripture declares, *"And ye shall know the truth, and **the truth shall make you free**"* (John 8:32).

Day 16: Power Prayer

Heavenly Father, I thank You for who You are and all that You have done in my life. Your Word is the final authority in my life, and Your Word says that You have not given me a spirit of fear, but of power and love, and of a sound mind. I declare that I am fearless in Jesus' name. I will not succumb to fear, cowardice, terror, or intimidation. I possess the mind of Christ, and Christ never operated in a victim mentality; therefore, I walk in bold faith and confidence in every area of my life. I am not a victim; I am a victor in Christ! Fear has no place is my thoughts or emotions in the name of Jesus. The Word of God declares, *"So then **faith cometh by hearing**, and hearing by the word of God"* (Romans 10:17). I am a hearer of the Word of God, therefore; I have great faith. Faith is the revelation of God's Word in action; therefore, I am a doer of Your Word and not just a hearer. No weapon formed against me shall prosper, including fear, worry, or dread. I life up the shield of faith and neutralize every fiery dart of fear and timidity in the name of Jesus. I declare that all irrational thoughts and phobias must leave me now in Jesus' name. I have no fear because the Lord is the strength of my life and my salvation.

55

Day 17: Unlocking the Heavens

Prove me now herewith, saith the LORD of hosts, if I will not open you the windows of heaven, and pour you out a blessing, that there shall not be room enough to receive it.
(Malachi 3:10)

In the Bible, the heavens are a very significant focal point of society and of religious worship. The heavens denote the source of God's favor, abundance, and prosperity. This is why the idiomatic expression "open the heavens" is used frequently throughout the Scriptures to denote God's favor being released upon a particular people during a particular season. Similarly, when the heavens are opened over our lives, there is a release of God's unmerited favor and miraculous power.

So what part do we play in all of this? The Bible says, *"And I will give unto thee the keys of the kingdom of heaven: and whatsoever thou shalt bind on earth shall be bound in heaven: and whatsoever thou shalt loose on earth shall be loosed in heaven"* (Matthew 16:19). Every time we pray in the earth, there is a response in the heavens. If you want to open the heavens above, you must open your heart and mouth in the earthly realm. Release God's powerful Word into the atmosphere. Pray in faith, and heaven will respond. Declare, "I walk under an open heaven in every area of my life in Jesus' name." Now that you have spoken the Word of God, the next step is to obey it. Obedience releases God's promises into your life.

Day 17: Power Prayer

Father, I thank You for Your goodness and grace that You have manifested in my life. I declare that Your favor surrounds me like a shield and that I walk in supernatural abundance in every area of my life. I live under an open heaven! You said, whatever I bind on earth is bound in heaven; therefore, I bind all lack, hindrance, stagnation, delay, poverty, ill-favor, and spiritual blockage operating in my life. I come into agreement and divine alignment with the culture of heaven. I loose peace and prosperity over my life and the lives of those who are connected with me. I command the devouring spirit to leave me now. I declare that Your Word will not return void, but it will accomplish what You have sent it to do in my life. Thank You, Lord, that Your blessings make rich and add no pain. This is my season of open doors, new opportunities, blessings, and divine arrangements. Thank You, Lord, that Your angels have been dispatched to my location, and they are fully prepared and equipped to bring the supernatural provision necessary for me to accomplish the assignment You have given me. I declare that I walk in unlimited obedience to Your Word, and therefore I am positioned to receive the supernatural rain of heaven in my life. Amen!

57

Day 18: Your Harvest Is Here!

*And let us not be weary in well doing: for in due season we
shall reap, if we faint not.* (Galatians 6:9)

Many people grow impatient with their season of life and
ask the Lord, "When will my time come?" Maybe you can
identify with this loaded question. Well, let me assure you: whatever you sow, you will reap. When I was growing up, I loved visiting
my grandmother's farm, which was always full of vegetables, fruits,
and animals. My grandmother knew how to take advantage of her
produce! She would always welcome me with fresh buttermilk biscuits with homemade butter and homemade peach preserves on
top, all of which was painstakingly prepared. I learned to appreciate not just her food but also the slow process the food had to go
through before I could enjoy it.

Like food slowly grown on a farm, you have been going
through God's agricultural process. Ultimately, He wants the
best out of your life. But many people become exhausted in the
process, oftentimes right before they are about to reap their
harvest. The Bible says, however, *"Let us not be weary in well doing…."* The word *"weary"* means "to be utterly spiritless, to be
wearied out, exhausted."

Don't be weary! I believe that your due season has come
upon you. I believe that your harvest is already here. It is time
for you to stand in faith, open your spiritual eyes, and prepare to
reap. This is not the season to be discouraged. What the enemy

meant to wear you out, God is going to use to "preserve" you! Just like my grandmother knew how to get the best use out of the fruits and vegetables on her farm, God knows how to get the best out of your life. Don't be exhausted! Don't give in to what your life may look like on the outside. God promises to prepare a table for you in the presence of your enemy. (See Psalm 23:5.) God is saying to you, "Your harvest is here!"

Day 18: Power Prayer

Father, in the name of Jesus, I thank You for who You are and all that You have done in my life. I recognize that You are a good God, and through Jesus, You have given me all things to enjoy. Your Word says that I should not be weary in well-doing, for I will reap a harvest if I do not faint. I declare that I will reap the harvest that You have prepared for me. I will not faint! I declare that I have supernatural endurance and perseverance in the things of God. Today, my harvest season has come upon me, and I am ready to receive all that You have prepared for my life. I refuse to complain, be bitter, or operate in discontented offense in this season because I know that those things produce stagnation. I bless my enemies as an act of faith, knowing that You prepare a table before me in the presence of my enemies. I declare that the blessings of God pursue me and overtake me right now. I prophesy a shift in the spiritual atmosphere of my life. I declare that the past seasons of drought, frustration, and toiling are over. I enter into a new season, a season of abundance and wholeness in the name of Jesus. Thank You, Lord, for Your abundant harvest. Amen!

Day 19: Binding *and* Loosing

*And I will give unto thee the keys of the kingdom of heaven:
and whatsoever thou shalt bind on earth shall be bound in
heaven: and whatsoever thou shalt loose on earth shall be
loosed in heaven.* (Matthew 16:19)

On my first trip to Israel, I had the wonderful opportunity to visit Caesarea Philippi, an ancient city rebuilt by Philip the Tetrarch during the first century. This city was known for pagan worship and happened to be the same place that Jesus asked His disciples the profound question, *"Whom do men say that I...am?"* (Matthew 16:13). This was a very bold question to ask His disciples, and Caesarea Philippi was an even bolder place to ask it. Peter answered Jesus and said, *"Thou art the Christ, the Son of the living God"* (verse 16). It was this revelation that initiated the proclamation of the authority of the church. Jesus told the disciples, *"And I will give unto you the keys of the kingdom of heaven...."* Notice in these verses the divine connection between identity and spiritual authority. Once we discover who Jesus is, we discover who we are, that we are positioned to exercise spiritual authority in the earth, and that we have been given the authority to bind and loose things in the heavenly realm.

What does it mean, exactly, to bind and to loose? The word *"bind"* comes from the Greek word *deō*, which means to "fasten, tie, forbid, or prohibit." The word *"loose"* comes from the Greek word *lyō*, which means "to undo, dissolve, release, or unbind." Whatever we prohibit on earth is prohibited or forbidden in heaven, and whatever we allow or permit in earth is permitted in heaven.

Like all tools, it doesn't matter how powerful binding and loosing are if you never use them. When was the last time you actually utilized the keys that you have been given? When was the last time you took authority over whatever the enemy was doing in your life? The keys are in your hand, and now it is time for you to use them!

Day 19: Power Prayer

Farther, I thank You for Your magnificent power working in and through my life. Today, I declare that You are the King of Kings and Lord of Lords. You are the Monarch of the universe. Through the blood of Jesus Christ, I have received the adoption of spiritual son/daughter. This relationship with You (through the blood of Jesus) gives me the right and authority to exercise spiritual dominion. You said that I have the keys of the kingdom of heaven; therefore, I declare that every demonic force, hindering spirit, and any other spiritual activity in the atmosphere that is contrary to Your divine purpose is bound and broken in Jesus' name. I release supernatural peace in my life. I declare that every demonic signal being transmitted by the enemy is disrupted in the name of Jesus. I loose prosperity, favor, increase, and healing over every area in my life and the lives of my loved ones. From this day forward, I operate in kingdom authority. I will never again be a victim of my circumstances! In Jesus' name, amen.

Day 20: The Power of Proclamation

And Jesus answering saith unto them, Have faith in God.
For verily I say unto you, that whosoever shall say unto
this mountain, Be thou removed, and be thou cast into the
sea; and shall not doubt in his heart, but shall believe that
those things which he saith shall come to pass; he shall have
whatsoever he saith. (Mark 11:22–23)

When God created Adam in the garden of Eden, one of the first assignments He gave Adam was to name the animals. This was no easy task! In the Hebrew context, names were very significant; they denoted purpose, function, and destiny. By naming the animals, Adam was exercising dominion in the garden of Eden. In the same way, you and I must exercise dominion in the world we live in through the words we speak. Adam was just following in the "footsteps" of his Creator and heavenly Father. God named every celestial being in the created universe, even the sun and the moon. In the midst of darkness, God proclaimed, *"Let there be light!"* (Genesis 1:3). By speaking light into the darkness, God was exercising dominion over the darkness. Similarly, we must exercise dominion over every area in our lives by speaking God's Word. This is what I call divine proclamation.

Jesus, in the eleventh chapter of Mark, spoke to the fig tree, and by the next day, it withered and died. Peter was puzzled by this marvelous phenomenon, and Jesus responded by saying, *"Have faith in God!"* This can also be translated, "Have the God kind of faith!" As we looked at before, He went further to say that *"whosoever shall say unto this mountain, Be thou removed, and be thou cast into the sea; and shall not doubt in his heart, but shall believe that those things which he saith shall come to pass; he shall have whatsoever he saith."* The word for *"say"* in this passage comes from the Greek word *legō,* which means "to teach or name." God has called us to name the things in our lives through the proclamation of His Word. Every time we speak, we are shaping the world around us and teaching things their function and purpose in our lives. I bet you never looked at things from that perspective before! What are you naming the circumstances in your life? Whatever name you call them will be their name and identity!

Day 20: Power Prayer

Father, I thank You for who You are and all that You have done in my life. I thank You, heavenly Father, for Your goodness and unmerited favor that surrounds me daily. Just as Adam named the animals in the garden of Eden, thus exercising dominion over his environment, I exercise spiritual dominion over my environment by proclaiming Your unadulterated Word over my life. I declare that I am the righteousness of God in Christ. I have authority over the enemy. I speak to every mountain (in every form and manifestation) and command them to move in the name of Jesus. I declare that despair, defeat, depression, and dejection have no place in my mind or in my life. I am healed, delivered, restored, and made whole by the power of the blood of Jesus. I declare that my children, family members, coworkers, and friends are blessed. I declare that I walk in total-life prosperity. By the grace of God, I reign in life. Situations and circumstances do not take dominion over me, but rather I take dominion over them. Amen!

Day 21: Too Blessed to Be Stressed

And God said unto Balaam, Thou shalt not go with them; thou shalt not curse the people: for they are blessed.

(Numbers 22:12)

No matter what sphere of influence or area of vocation you operate in, you have probably encountered some form of stress. In fact, according to the American Institute of Stress, 77 percent of Americans experience physical symptoms related to stress! Is this the will of God for the believer? Many years ago, I heard the expression "Too blessed to be stressed!" Even if it seems a little cheesy, I love this phrase! It reminds me that God has been too good for me to complain or worry about the circumstances of my life.

In the book of Numbers, God told the backslidden prophet Balaam not to curse Israel, because they were a blessed people. The word *"blessed"* here is the Hebrew word *barak*, which means (among other things) to "be blessed, to kneel, or to be adored." It means to "be endowed with divine favor, protection, and prosperity." Look at how powerful this idea of blessing becomes in the New Testament: *"Christ hath redeemed us from the curse of the law, being made a curse for us: for it is written, Cursed is every one that hangeth on a tree: that the blessing of Abraham might come on the Gentiles through Jesus Christ; that we might receive the promise of the Spirit through faith"* (Galatians 3:13–14).

Through Christ, you and I have received the blessing of Abraham. We are no longer under the curse! In other words, we have been empowered to prosper, and we have been endowed with the favor and goodness of God. It doesn't matter what things look like in your life; God says you are blessed. Why, then, are so many believers' lives filled with frustration, stress, and worry? They are simply not aware of the full ramifications of the blessing. As new covenant believers, we have no business operating in worry or frustration. Some might say, "But everyone has to be stressed sometimes!" Says who? Jesus told us to take no thought for our lives. He told us not to worry about anything! We are too blessed to be stressed!

Day 21: Power Prayer

Father, in the name of Jesus, I thank You for who You are and all that You have done. Today, I declare in the name of Jesus Christ that I am stress-free. Worry and anxiety do not have permission to occupy my mind. I cast all of my cares and concerns on Jesus Christ, for He cares for me. (See 1 Peter 5:7.) I am worry-free and stress-free today! Nothing will separate me from the peace and love of God. I dwell in the *shalom* of God in every area of my life; there is nothing missing and nothing broken. I declare that rivers of supernatural peace flood my soul and mind right now. You said that You would keep him in perfect peace whose mind is stayed on You (see Isaiah 26:3); therefore, I declare that I have perfect peace! The peace of God resonates within my inner being. Nothing has the power or ability to disturb my internal atmosphere. Father, I will walk and thrive in the blessing of Abraham, which You have placed upon my life. I am blessed beyond measure, and there is not a demon, witch, warlock, or agent of darkness capable of cursing me, because I am blessed in the name of Jesus. Amen!

69

Day 22: The Spirit of Intercession

Wherefore he is able also to save them to the uttermost that come unto God by him, seeing he ever liveth to make intercession for them.   (Hebrews 7:25)

When I was growing up in church, I often heard the term "intercession" or "intercessor." At the time, I took this to mean "an old woman who was more spiritual than anyone else in the church and who prayed for everyone else, including the pastor." Your perception of "intercessor" might not be quite that specific, but there does seem to be a general consensus among believers that intercession is not for everyone. Nothing could be further than the truth! The truth is that intercession is the responsibility and privilege of *every* New Testament believer.

So what is intercession? The word "*intercession*" comes from the Greek word *entygchanō*, which means "to fall in with, to meet a person, converse, consult, or to entreat." Actually, intercession is a legal term that denotes consulting with someone on behalf of another. One of the most powerful spiritual weapons given to the New Testament believer is intercession: the right and responsibility to go before God on behalf of another. Paul encouraged believers to intercede: *"Praying always with all prayer and supplication in the Spirit, and watching thereunto with all perseverance and supplication for all saints"* (Ephesians 6:18).

Now, we know that Jesus Christ is the ultimate Intercessor, who went to God on our behalf and with His blood purged us from sin; however, we have a responsibility (as those who have been redeemed) to pray for those who cannot pray for themselves. Sometimes, while you are praying, you may feel a burden to pray for somebody in particular. This is what we call the spirit of intercession. God has called you and me to be watchmen on the wall. He wants us to pray for others under the inspiration and unction of the Holy Spirit. The more you engage in prayer for others, the more you, along with those you are praying with and for, will receive healing. This is why James wrote, *"Confess your faults one to another, and pray one for another, **that ye may be healed**. The effectual fervent prayer of a righteous man availeth much"* (James 5:16). The enemy's agenda is to get you so caught up in your own problems that you don't have the time or energy to pray for others. The devil is a liar! Give him no place! Pray for one another!

71

Day 22: Power Prayer

Father, in the name of Jesus, I thank You for Your everlasting goodness and love toward me. Two thousand years ago, Christ died on the cross for my sins, redeeming me from the curse of the law and placing me in a position of righteousness. Through the blood of Jesus, I have been made a king and a priest unto God, and given the priestly ministry of intercession. Today, I take my place as a prophetic intercessor on behalf of my family, friends, and loved ones. I declare that my loved ones have a real and genuine relationship with God, through Jesus Christ. I declare that all curses and spiritual hindrances are broken off of them in the name of Jesus. I release Your miraculous healing power into the lives of my family, my community, and my network of friends. I pray for those who would consider themselves my enemies, and I bless them with all of my heart. I make intercession for those in a position of authority including kings, presidents, governors, magistrates, and pastors. Cover their families and bless them with divine health and soundness of mind, I pray. I declare that all attacks from the enemy against their destiny are neutralized and broken in Jesus' name. Amen!

Day 23: Deliverance Prayers

That if thou shalt confess with thy mouth the Lord Jesus, and shalt believe in thine heart that God hath raised him from the dead, thou shalt be saved. For with the heart man believeth unto righteousness; and with the mouth confession is made unto salvation. (Romans 10:9–10)

Whether people realize it and want to admit it or not, Christians need deliverance. I have heard it said on many occasions that a Christian couldn't have a demon. This is simply not true, because it is not biblical. Many times in the New Testament, when it talks about casting out a demon, it was not referring to someone who was *possessed* by a demon but to someone who was *oppressed* by a demon. While it is true that a born-again believer cannot be possessed (that is, owned or controlled) by a demon, it is very possible for them to be under demonic oppression.

For example, the gospel of Luke gives an account of a woman under demonic oppression: *"And, behold, there was a woman which had a spirit of infirmity eighteen years, and was bowed together, and could in no wise lift up herself. And when Jesus saw her, he called her to him, and said unto her, Woman, thou art loosed from thine infirmity. And he laid his hands on her: and immediately she was made straight, and glorified God"* (Luke 13:11–13). A spirit of infirmity, which affected her ability to walk upright, was oppressing this woman. Jesus used the expression, *"Thou art loosed,*" which comes from the Greek word *apolyō*, meaning "to set free, to let go, or to dismiss." This woman was delivered from an evil spirit! Most believers don't think of sickness as an unclean spirit, but it can be in many instances. In fact, the word *"saved"* in Romans 10 also means, "delivered" or "set free." We have been delivered, we are being delivered, and we will be delivered. I want to take a moment and lead you in some deliverance prayers that will enable you to experience greater levels of victory and joy in your life.

Day 23: Power Prayer

For Emotional Bondage: Father, in the name of Jesus, I take authority over any and all forms of emotional bondage, confusion, or turmoil in the name of Jesus Christ. I declare that I am free from spirits of calamity and chaos in Jesus' name. The Word of God declares that the peace of God rules my heart and mind through Christ Jesus; therefore, I loose myself from the plans and schemes of the evil one. Amen!

For Fear: The Word of God declares that I have not received a spirit of fear, but of power, love, and soundness of mind; therefore, I declare that any and all fear must leave my soul and my body *right now* in the name of Jesus!

For Perversion and Addictions: Father, I thank You for who You are and all that You have done in my life. I believe that Jesus Christ is Your Son; I believe He suffered on the cross and died, defeating the wicked one

74

in hell. I believe that Jesus Christ was raised from the dead and is now seated at the right hand of God making intercession for me. Today, I give You, Jesus, complete control of my life. I ask that You forgive me of any and all sin, and that You cleanse me from all unrighteousness. I repent of all sins, known and unknown. I declare that Jesus Christ is my Lord and Savior. I expose my entire spirit, soul, and body to the blood of Jesus Christ, the Word of God, and the fire of the Holy Spirit, and I command anything in me that was not planted by the Lord Jesus to be uprooted in Jesus' name.

For Sickness: Thank You, Lord, for the blood of Jesus Christ which cleanses me of all sin and restores me to a position of righteousness in You. In 1 Peter 2:24 it says, *"Who his own self bare our sins in his own body on the tree, that we, being dead to sins, should live unto righteousness: by whose stripes ye were healed."* Therefore, I declare that I was completely healed two thousand years ago, and sickness no longer has a legal right to operate in my body. The law of the Spirit of Life in Christ Jesus has made me free from the law of sin and death; therefore, I declare that sickness cannot reign in my mortal body. My body is the temple of the Holy Spirit, and I drive out all sickness, disease, and infirmity. I am totally and completely healed! Amen!

Day 24: Greater Is He!

*Ye are of God, little children, and have overcome them: because **greater is he** that is in you, than he that is in the world.* (1 John 4:4)

Have you taken the time lately to consider the magnitude and magnificence of the One who lives within you? Did you know that the Creator of the universe dwells on the inside of you (if you are born again)? This means that you should never allow yourself to be victimized by your circumstances again! Meditate on the fact that the Spirit dwells in you: *"But **if the Spirit of him that raised up Jesus from the dead dwell** in you, he that raised up Christ from the dead shall also quicken your mortal bodies by his Spirit that dwelleth in you"* (Romans 8:11). In other words, we have resurrection power dwelling within. The word "dwell" comes from the Greek word *enoikeō*, which means "to dwell in one and influence him."

Have you ever seen a submarine? How is a submarine able to descend thousands of feet into the ocean? If a person tried to dive a thousand feet without any special equipment or vessel, their body would literally be crushed by the weight of the water above them. However, a submarine is pressurized, and therefore able to withstand the pressure of the ocean. Why? The pressure within the submarine is greater than the ocean's pressure on the outside.

This is also true of the believer! The power, presence, and anointing on the inside of you is *greater* than any trials, temptations, or tribulations that the world's system can bring against you. In essence, the Spirit of the living God has pressurized you! You don't need to fear or worry. There is enough power on the inside of you to overcome anything or anyone that is coming against you. Instead of caving in under pressure, be the spiritual submarine that God has called you to be, buoyant, full of faith and power.

Day 24: Power Prayer

Father, I thank You for the power of Your Word. Through Your Son, Jesus Christ, I have been redeemed from the curse and made the righteousness of God in Him. Your Word declares that greater is He who lives in me than he who lives in the world; therefore, I declare that I am more than a conqueror through Him who loves me. I am full of supernatural power, anointing, victory, and heavenly wisdom. There is no situation or circumstance in my life than I cannot overcome, because I can do all things through Christ (the Anointed One and His anointing), which gives me strength. (See Philippians 4:13.) I am strong in You, Lord, and in the power of Your might! Demons tremble when my name is mentioned, because I am a joint heir with Jesus Christ. I refuse to cave in or succumb to the pressures of this life, because I have been pressurized with supernatural power and ability in every area of my life. I declare that I walk in freedom, power, and victory. I declare that no weapon fashioned against me by the evil one will be able to prevail. I declare that all of the attacks of the devil are neutralized in my life. Thank You, Lord, for Your mighty power that works in and through me in the name of Jesus. Amen!

Day 25: Good Versus Evil

And the Lord God commanded the man, saying, Of every tree of the garden thou mayest freely eat: but of the tree of the knowledge of good and evil, thou shalt not eat of it: for in the day that thou eatest thereof thou shalt surely die.
(Genesis 2:16–17)

*But strong meat belongeth to them that are of full age, even those who by reason of use have their **senses exercised** to discern both good and evil.*   (Hebrews 5:14)

Ever since we were children, we've been taught about what's right and what's wrong. Doing the dishes is right. Touching the hot stove is wrong. I even remember my parents trying to teach me the difference between good friends and bad friends. When Adam and Eve were in the garden of Eden, God instructed them not to eat from the Tree of the Knowledge of Good and Evil because that was wrong. Before the fall, Adam and Eve were only conscious of their relationship with God; they had no conception of right versus wrong, except for the eating of the tree. However, after Eve took from the tree (under the temptation of the serpent) and ate its fruit, then gave to Adam to eat, they became "sin conscious." As a result of this, mankind must now distinguish between good and evil in this world.

When God does away with this present world's system, we will no longer need to be aware of the difference between good and evil, but in the meantime it is a very important for us to make this distinction. In the book of Hebrews, the writer tells us that mature believers have the ability to distinguish good from evil. Many believers, however, are not skilled in understanding the difference between good and evil. In fact, many people refer to evil things as good and to good things as evil. Beloved, this is not the will of God for your life. He wants you to be mature in spiritual things. Part of our prophetic DNA is the capacity to discern good from evil. Whether it is opportunities, life choices, or career decisions, you and I need to be able to have clarity on what is of God and what is not of God. As believers, we are responsible for exercising our senses by praying and meditating on the Word of God.

Day 25: Power Prayer

Lord, this world is a confusing place! Lord, I thank You that You are the very definition of everything that is good, and yet, Lord, I confess that I find it difficult to discern between right and wrong, good and evil. Activate my senses, Lord, so that I might know what is of You. Lord, I declare that I have the maturity of faith to make the right decisions in my life. I declare that the wisdom from above is inside my heart, guiding me every minute of the day. I declare that nothing is too big for You, and nothing is too small; therefore, I dedicate every single decision, every single word, and every single action to You. I seek to discern what is of You. Guide my meditation and study of Your Word, so that I might see with the eyes of faith and look with maturity at my life, for Your glory and in the name of Jesus Christ. Amen!

81

Day 26: Don't Stop!

*Ye did **run well**; who did hinder you that ye should not obey the truth?* (Galatians 5:7)

Elijah the prophet, whom we've met before, engages in an infamous showdown with the prophets of Baal in the book of 1 Kings. As Elijah prayed, the fire of God, the true God of Israel, descended upon the altars of Baal, the false god, consuming the sacrifices and causing onlookers to marvel at the omnipotent power of God. After this powerful display, Elijah killed the prophets of Baal: *"And the hand of the LORD was on Elijah; and he girded up his loins, and ran before Ahab to the entrance of Jezreel"* (1 Kings 18:46). Elijah began to run so fast that he outran King Ahab's chariot. Talk about horsepower! This was another supernatural manifestation of God.

But when Jezebel, the queen, found out about all the great exploits that Elijah performed under the power of God, she threatened to kill him as a consequence of his actions. You would think that the mighty prophet of God would have responded, "Thus saith the Lord, you do not intimidate me, woman!" Instead, the prophet flees from Jezreel, and hides under a juniper tree, terrified for his life. The reader of 1 Kings is left puzzled! What about all the miracles he just performed? What about all the power that was demonstrated? Well, Elijah had had an awesome run, but he was now hindered by a serious spiritual attack.

Does this sound familiar? Many people have lost their spiritual momentum because of an attack from the enemy. They have stopped moving forward in their purpose and assignment. This attack can take the form of sickness, disease, discouragement, fear, or any other weapon the enemy chooses from his arsenal to cause you to stop running for God. This is what I call a "juniper tree moment." It was under the juniper tree that God reminded Elijah that he was not alone, and that the assignment he was given was still valid. God is saying to you today, "You are not alone, and your assignment is still valid!" So come out from under that juniper of despair and discouragement and "run on" for the Lord. Don't stop!

Day 26: Power Prayer

Father, in the name of Jesus, I thank You for the power of Your Word. I thank You for Your goodness and grace, which You have continually shown me. Today, I declare that I operate in divine momentum. I declare that I consistently operate and function in my divine assignment, and I move in my supernatural purpose. I refuse to yield to the evil reports or intimidating tactics of the evil one. Instead, I will run on tirelessly for the Lord, in the name of Jesus! Amen.

Day 27: Destiny Acceleration

For I know the thoughts that I think toward you, saith the
LORD, thoughts of peace, and not of evil, to give you an
expected end.   (Jeremiah 29:11)

What is destiny? "Destiny" is defined as the hidden power believed to control what will happen in the future. In Jeremiah 29, the Bible records: *"For I know the thoughts that I think toward you, saith the LORD."* The word *"thoughts"* in Hebrew means "plans or purpose." God has a purpose and a plan for our lives. When most people think about destiny, they think of something that is guaranteed to happen in the future, regardless of their decisions or actions. Nothing could be further from the truth. We have a very important part to play in God's plan for our lives. In the case of the Israelites in the book of Jeremiah, their ability to walk in the fullness of God's purpose was contingent on their faith and obedience to the Word of God. The same is true of you and me. Every time we pray in faith and act on the promises of God, we actually *accelerate our destiny*. In other words, you aren't waiting on God; He is waiting on you!

Have you ever felt as if your life was moving in the right direction? Or, on the other hand, have you ever felt a certain level of stagnation? The Scripture says that God desires to bring you to an expected end. God has an end in mind when He looks at your life. This end is a hopeful end; one filled with peace, prosperity, and victory. You have been predestinated to victory and success. Now that you know what's on God's mind concerning your future, it is time for you to align your thoughts, words, and actions with His thoughts. It is time for you and me to pray His purposes into manifestation and thereby accelerate our destinies. This is not magic! It is being intentional about seeing God's promises come to pass in your life. Don't wait! Open your mouth and release your destiny!

Day 27: Power Prayer

Father, in the name of Jesus, I thank You that Your plans for my life are good and not evil. You desire to bring me to an expected end, and to give me a hope and a future. Your Word declares, in Psalm 5:12, that Your favor surrounds me like a shield. Thank You for Your everlasting goodness and grace toward me. I declare that I am hopeful concerning my future, because of the precious and unfailing promises I read in Your Word. I will never look to my future with cynicism, negativity, or fear ever again. I declare that it is well concerning my future! My future looks brighter and brighter, because You are the one leading and guiding me. I know that Your plan for me is good, and that the days ahead will be filled with peace and prosperity. Right now, I align my thoughts, words, prayers, and actions with the agenda of heaven for my life. I declare that Your purposes and plans are made manifest in my life *today*! I am excited about my future, and I look forward to my tomorrow with confidence, expectancy, anticipation, and joy. I declare that I will realize every aspect of the destiny that You have ordained for my life, including my ministry, family, finances, relationships, and overall quality of life, in Jesus' name! Amen!

Day 28: The Spirit of Python

And it came to pass, as we went to prayer, a certain damsel possessed with a spirit of divination met us, which brought her masters much gain by soothsaying…And this did she many days. But Paul, being grieved, turned and said to the spirit, I command thee in the name of Jesus Christ to come out of her. And he came out the same hour.

(Acts 16:16, 18)

These verses present us with a very interesting scenario. Paul and Silas find themselves followed and taunted by a woman possessed with a spirit of divination. After several days, Paul finally became fed up with her taunting and mockery, and cast the demon out of her. Praise the Lord! The irony is that this woman was speaking things concerning Paul that were true, but she was speaking them in the wrong spirit. In fact, the Bible makes specific reference to the spirit of divination. What was this? The word *"divination"* here literally means "python," referring to Apollo, also called "Pythius," a false god who held much sway over the Grecian beliefs. But think about the imagery here. A python is a large, heavy-bodied, nonvenomous constrictor snake that kills its prey by wrapping itself around and around them until they're strangled. The spirit in this woman (or upon this woman) was a python spirit. Just as the name signifies, the python spirit attempts to choke the life out of believers by oppressing their body, mind, emotions, and spiritual life. Chronic sickness, fear, addictions, and emotional turmoil are just a few manifestations of this evil spirit.

The Bible says that Paul was *"grieved"* by this spirit. The word "grieved" comes from the Greek word *diaponeomai*, which means "to be troubled, displeased, offended, pained, to be worked up." In short, Paul became tired of this spirit! If you and I are going to walk in total freedom from the spirit of python, we have to come to a place in our heart and mind where enough is enough! It is not the will of God for believers to live under oppression and bondage. If you or a loved one are being tormented by a spirit of python, simply do what Paul did and say, "I command thee in the name of Jesus Christ to leave." Take authority over the enemy! Satan has no right to mock, frustrate, torment, or oppress you or anyone you love.

Day 28: Power Prayer

Heavenly Father, I thank You for breaking the power of the spirit of python over my life and the lives of those I love. Your Word declares that You have given me authority over all the power of the enemy and that nothing shall by any means hurt me. Right now, in Jesus' name, I declare that I am completely free from any and all addictions, perversions, compulsions, oppressions, fears, and life-controlling issues. I loose myself (and those I love) from the demonic stranglehold of the spirit of python and command all depression, anxiety, fear, and chronic sickness to leave my spirit, soul, and body right now in Jesus' name! Devil, I loose myself from you and I command you to leave me now! He whom the Son shall make free is free indeed; therefore, I declare my complete and total freedom from this day forward in Jesus' name. I no longer have to live under the grief and distress of a spirit of oppression. I declare that all my loved ones, friends, and coworkers are also delivered from the demonic influence of this evil spirit. In the name of Jesus Christ of Nazareth, I declare the spirit of python broken off my life once and for all. Amen!

Day 29: The Blood of the Lamb

Forasmuch as ye know that ye were not redeemed with corruptible things, as silver and gold, from your vain conversation received by tradition from your fathers; but with the precious blood of Christ, as of a lamb without blemish and without spot: who verily was foreordained before the foundation of the world, but was manifest in these last times for you. (1 Peter 1:18–20)

O ne of the most significant holy days in the Old Testament was Yom Kippur, or the Day of Atonement. During this sacred time, the High Priest would take a scapegoat and lay his hands on it, symbolically transferring the sins of the entire nation of Israel onto the animal. Then the High Priest would banish the goat into the wilderness, representing the putting away of Israel's sin before God. After that, a spotless lamb would be sacrificed, representing the atoning (expiating) of Israel's sin, and thus cleansing the entire nation of their iniquities. To this very day, Yom Kippur is the most holy day in Israel.

However, Yom Kippur was just a type and shadow of something much more powerful. Two thousand years ago, Jesus Christ became both the Scapegoat and the sacrificial Lamb, sacrificing Himself of the cross of Calvary for the sins of the entire world (not just the nation of Israel), so that all who believe in Him may be redeemed from the curse of sin, and stand clean, forgiven, and justified before a holy God. What a wonderful display of God's goodness! The blood of Jesus Christ has cleansed every born-again believer from their sins, and has transformed us into new creations.

When I was growing up, my mother would use bleach to remove heavy stains from clothing. Depending on how soiled the clothing was, there would sometimes still be a remnant of the original stain. In contrast, the blood of Jesus Christ removes any and all stains and leaves no trace of our iniquities, but washes us completely clean. Hallelujah! The blood of Jesus Christ is more powerful than anything you have ever imagined. It was the only ransom worthy of redeeming us. No matter what you are dealing with in your life, you must recognize that the blood of Jesus Christ is more than able to redeem, heal, deliver, and cleanse you. There is power in the blood!

Day 29: Power Prayer

Father, in the name of Jesus Christ, I thank You for the blood of Jesus. Through your shed blood, I have been redeemed from the curse of the law of sin and death. According to Galatians 3:13–14, You became a curse for me and hung on the tree so that I might receive the blessing of Abraham. Thank You, Jesus, for fulfilling Yom Kippur on my behalf. The Word of God declares that the life is in the blood. You exchanged Your life for mine and paid my ransom. I receive the blood sacrifice that You made for me, and I know that though You I am completely clean and justified. I declare that the blood of Jesus Christ neutralizes every curse. I declare that the blood of Jesus Christ is the title deed for my healing, deliverance, and breakthrough. I serve notice to the kingdom of darkness that the blood of Jesus is against it! The enemy can no longer condemn, accuse, or slander my name because my sins are under the blood of Jesus. Thank You, Lord, for Your mighty power working in and through my life. Just as the blood of bulls and goats had power under the old covenant to atone and bring restoration, so Your blood, as the ultimate payment, has the power to completely restore my total self. The blood of Jesus covers me in every area of my life. Amen!

Day 30: Supernatural Breakthrough

And at midnight Paul and Silas prayed, and sang praises unto God: and the prisoners heard them. And suddenly there was a great earthquake, so that the foundations of the prison were shaken: and immediately all the doors were opened, and every one's bands were loosed.

(Acts 16:25–26)

I don't know about you, but it seems to me that every believer at some point during their life needs to experience a spiritual breakthrough. What do I mean by spiritual breakthrough? Well, a spiritual breakthrough is when God intervenes supernaturally on our behalf—when He comes through and manifests Himself in a mighty way in our lives.

For a famous example, think of Paul and Silas, who, as Acts 16 recounts, were imprisoned after they had cast the spirit of python out of a woman. As a result of this courageous act, the enemy retaliated. Have you ever experienced demonic retaliation? When you do something according to the will of God, the enemy tries to make you pay for it. It is in these moments, just as Paul and Silas experienced, that you and I need to release our faith to experience a breakthrough in our lives.

I believe that God is about to manifest His power in and through your life like never before. All you have to do is maintain an attitude of faith and expectancy, and you will posture yourself to experience the miraculous. This is exactly what happened in the case of Paul and Silas. Instead of complaining and being frustrated with God over what He allowed to touch their lives, they chose to give God glory: *"And at midnight Paul and Silas prayed, and sang praises unto God."*

Is this your attitude? We all must have a "midnight" experience, where things seem to look dark and hopeless. But these are the best, the most important times to pray and sing praises to God, because you know that He is more than able to break through into your life: *"And suddenly there was a great earthquake, so that the foundations of the prison were shaken: and immediately all the doors were opened, and every one's bands were loosed."* God is about to shake your foundations, open supernatural doors, and loose you from everything that had you bound, in Jesus' name. This is your time for supernatural breakthrough!

Day 30: Power Prayer

Father, in the name of Jesus, I thank You for who You are and all that You have done. Thank You, Lord, for being my Deliverer. Thank You, Lord, for being the Source of miraculous power in my life. I declare, in the name of Jesus, that all bondages, barriers, blockages, and hindrances in my life are released, and that the power of the enemy is broken. I declare that I walk in supernatural breakthrough in every area of my life. The Bible says that the anointing destroys the yoke; therefore, I decree and declare that every yoke is destroyed and every burden is removed in the name of Jesus. I refuse to be bound another day in my life! I declare that the goodness, favor, and anointing of God abound toward me. I refuse to complain, be frustrated, or angry with the Lord over the things that He has allowed in my life. Instead, I choose to praise, worship, pray, and give thanks for the goodness of God that He has displayed toward me. I declare that today is the day of my supernatural breakthrough in the name of Jesus. Amen!

Day 31: The Hearing of Faith

*He therefore that ministereth to you the Spirit, and worketh miracles among you, doeth he it by the works of the law, or by the **hearing of faith**?*　　　(Galatians 3:5)

My father was a military man, and some of his training showed up in how he raised me. Again and again as a boy, I was taught about the importance of listening to instructions. "Pay attention!" he would often emphasize, adding that I should be sure to listen more than I spoke. I discovered at an early age that hearing and listening were key to being successful in life.

Well, the same is true in the kingdom of God. Everything about our ability to manifest the supernatural is contingent upon our capacity to hear what the Holy Spirit is saying. The Bible tells us in Romans 10:17, *"Faith cometh by hearing, and hearing by the word of God."* The Greek word for *"hearing"* in this passage means "to understand, to perceive the sense of what is said." In other words, you and I have spiritual ears, and the more we understand or perceive the sense of the Word of God, more we will be positioned to experience the miraculous. This is what we call the hearing of faith. Yes, that's right, faith has ears!

The more we hear the Word of God, and get the Word of God down in our spirit, the more we will produce a harvest of the miraculous. If you are always listening to (and internalizing) things that are contrary to the Word of God, how then will you be able to release your faith for miracles? If you always surround yourself with naysayers and listen to their negativity, how can you believe in God to accomplish the impossible? On the other hand, if you begin to hear the Holy Spirit on a regular basis, meditating in and applying the Word of God to your life, you will begin to see change and transformation. If you want to see miracles, meditate on the miraculous. If you want to see healing, meditate on what the Word says about healing. Many people think that success in the Christian life is about following religious rituals, but nothing could be further from the truth. True success in the kingdom is a result of deep intimacy with the Holy Spirit and active faith in God's Word.

Day 31: Power Prayer

Father God, in the name of Jesus, I thank You for who You are and all that You have done. Lord, I thank You for opening my spiritual ears. I declare that I possess the hearing of faith. I have the supernatural ability to hear what the Holy Spirit is saying to me at all times. I declare that anything that is blocking or preventing me from hearing Your voice is removed right now. Your Word declares that Your sheep hear Your voice and a stranger they will not follow. (See John 10:27.) I will not follow the voice of a stranger! I will only follow the voice of the Holy Spirit, who speaks God's Word. I declare that I walk in miracles, signs, wonders. I declare that I receive divine wisdom in every area of my life. My spirit man is receptive to the Word of God. I will hear the Word, I will receive the Word, and I will do the Word. I declare that heaven downloads divine wisdom, witty inventions, and supernatural ideas to me on a regular basis. I declare that from this day forward, I possess the hearing of faith, and I walk in God's miraculous power. In the name of Jesus, amen!

Day 32: Marriage and Relationships

*Wherefore they are no more twain, but one flesh. What therefore God hath joined together, let not man put **asunder**.*
(Matthew 19:6)

Marriage is one of the most honorable and beautiful things that human beings can participate in. We know based on Scripture that marriage was the first institution of God. Paul also tells us in Ephesians 6 that marriage is a *type*, or a picture, of the relationship between Christ and His church. If marriage is the representation of Christ and the church, then you and I need to understand who Christ is in order to properly understand the marital relationship. Because Christ is the Word, and He is found in the Word, this should make us even more eager to study and meditate on the Word. (See, especially, the book of Ephesians.)

As with all good things created by God, however, the enemy has attempted to distort and pervert the marital union. I believe this is why we are seeing so many attacks on the marital dynamic all around us. When the enemy wants to destroy a society, he first attacks the family, and when he wants to destroy the family structure, he first attacks marriages. It is the will of God for you and I to have productive, prosperous, and successful marriages and relationships. Contrary to popular opinion, marriages and relationships are still very important to the Lord!

Maybe you have had some challenges in your marriage or in your relationships. Well, as prophetic intercessors, God has called us to be able to speak His Word and His will into our relationships. We have the divine capacity to set things in order according to the will of almighty God. If your relationships are not going the way that you believe they should, don't be frustrated; God has an answer for you. If He is the Manufacturer of all things, this means that He has the manual for everything that He created. The manual for marriage is the Word of God. If you make the decision that God's Word is the final authority, and submit to it, things *will* turn around in your relationships.

Day 32: Power Prayer for Marriage

100

Father, in the name of Jesus, I thank You for who You are and all that You have done. Lord, I thank You that I have a healthy marriage according to Your Word. I decree and declare that my marriage is well-pleasing to You in every aspect. I declare that I have a servant heart, and my ministry is to serve You, Lord, and to serve my spouse with a pure heart.

As a husband I declare that I love my wife with the love of Christ. I am the head of this union. I am the priest of this union. I follow You, Lord, as the Captain of my life, and in doing so, I am a faithful servant leader in my marriage relationship. I lay down my life for my wife on a consistent basis. I love my wife as Christ loved the church and gave Himself for it.

As a wife I decree and declare that I am a godly helper to my husband. I have a meek and quiet spirit. I am obedient to my husband as unto the Lord. I am a strong example of what a godly wife should be. I am virtuous and industrious as a Proverbs 31 woman. My marriage has perfect communication, perfect love, and perfect agreement in the name of Jesus Christ.

Day 32: Power Prayer for Relationships

Father, in the name of Jesus, I thank You for who You are and all that You have done. I decree right now that I am whole and complete. I thank You that I have healthy, godly relationships that consist of healthy and edifying boundaries. I thank You that I am connected with people that encourage my emotional, spiritual, and mental growth. I thank You that I am fully equipped to be a godly example in any circle of influence I am in. People who interact with me will be closer to God because of our interaction. I declare that *all* of my relationships are holy and Christ-like. I thank You that my friendships, partnerships, and family relationships bring You glory, in Jesus' name! Amen.

101

Day 33: The Mind of Christ

*For who hath known the mind of the Lord, that he may instruct him? But we have the **mind of Christ**.*

(1 Corinthians 2:16)

In my book *The Power of Prophetic Prayer,* I discuss the fact that every believer possesses a prophetic DNA. The Bible tells us that we have received the testimony of Jesus Christ, which is the spirit of prophecy. Paul goes even further and tells us that we have the mind of Christ. Have you ever heard the expression, "She has her father's brain," or "He has his father's eyes"? Such comments reflect what we call a genetic inheritance. In other words, there are things that we inherit from our parents that we didn't do anything to earn or deserve. These attributes are written into our genetic code.

Similarly, New Testament believers have inherited the very mind of our Lord Jesus. In the Greek, the word *"mind"* (*nous*) signifies the ability to perceive and understand or to judge and determine. You and I have received the Lord's ability to understand, perceive, judge, and determine situations and circumstances. This means that we are no longer supposed to think or perceive like the world does. We have access to the divine mind of Christ Himself. This is amazing! Jesus was never moved or exasperated by the circumstances around Him, because He was always conscious and aware of His heavenly Father. We no longer have to settle for the fragile, anxious, and worrisome mind that we received from our natural blood lineage because we have received a supernatural mind that is far more superior—a mind governed by the peace of God. We develop this mind through prayer, intercession, and meditation on God's Word.

I often tell people, "What you set your mind on, you will manifest!" Jesus walked in perfect, unsullied communion with God all the days of His life. Guess what? You have access to the same thing as a born-again believer in Jesus. What if I told you that you no longer had to be ruled or controlled by fear, confusion, and doubt? Well, you don't! You have the mind of Christ, and it is time for you to use it!

Day 33: Power Prayer

Father, in the name of Jesus, I thank You for who You are and all that You have done in my life. I declare that I possess this mind of Christ. Just as a child inherits the DNA of their biological father, I have inherited the spiritual DNA of my heavenly Father through Jesus Christ. I declare that anxiety, fear, worry, frustration, and confusion have no place in my mind. I declare that I think like Jesus, I reason like Jesus, I perceive like Jesus, and I understand like Jesus. I declare that I am not conformed to this world, but the renewing of my mind transforms me. With every passing moment, I think more like Jesus. I take dominion in my thought life, and I cast down every imagination that contradicts the knowledge of Jesus in my life. I declare that every mind-binding spirit is broken off of my mind, and I think with clarity, precision, and purpose. I thank You, Lord, that You are the Ruler of my mind and my life in Jesus' name. Amen!

Day 34: Positive Attitude

*Finally, brethren, whatsoever things are true, whatsoever things are honest, whatsoever things are just, whatsoever things are pure, whatsoever things are lovely, whatsoever things are of good report; if there be any virtue, and if there be any praise, **think on these things**.* (Philippians 4:8)

I heard a story one day about an elderly woman who lived in a nursing home. She had been a resident of this particular nursing facility for several years, and she had been in the same room the entire time she was there. One day, the management of the nursing home decided to shift the current layout to accommodate more residents. They decided to relocate Mrs. Grace to another room down the hall. When the orderlies came to move her to her new room, she was so excited. She told everyone that her new room was the most beautiful one she had ever seen. The orderly eventually replied, "Mrs. Grace, you haven't even seen the room yet, so how can you be so excited about it?" She said to him, "Son, I choose to be excited regardless of how it looks. I have already decided that it will be the best room I have ever had." That is what we call a positive attitude!

What is an attitude? An attitude is a settled way of thinking or feeling about someone or something, typically reflected in a person's behavior. Have you ever met someone that was always cynical and pessimistic? They see the glass as half empty rather than half full. In fact, the pessimist doesn't even like the color of the glass nor the quality of the water. This should not be true of the born-again believer! The Scriptures admonish us to think on things that are pure, lovely, and of a good report. How do you view people and circumstances? How do you view yourself? All of these things are a part of your mental attitude. Many people are not able to see blessings and favor in their lives, because they have a negative mind-set. They are always complaining about the circumstances of their lives. Beloved, this is not the way God intends for us to be. In fact, one of the main differences between prophetic people and pathetic people is their attitude. Remember, there is always something to complain about, but for every one negative thing in our lives, there are one hundred positive things to be grateful for.

Day 34: Power Prayer

Father, in the name of Jesus, I thank You for all that You have done in my life. I thank You for every blessing and opportunity that You have extended toward me. I know that You are good and Your mercy endures forever. I declare that I possess a positive mental attitude. I am appreciative and grateful for everything in my life. I refuse to be negative, cynical, or pessimistic about any circumstance or situation in my life. I am optimistic because I recognize Your good plan for my life. I declare that prosperity, favor, and open doors pursue me and overtake me. I declare that I have more than enough; I lack nothing! I am not governed, manipulated, or controlled by my circumstances, negative emotions, or the negative words and thoughts of others; instead, I dwell in the secret place of God's presence and abide under the shadow of His wings.

Day 35: Freedom from Depression

To appoint unto them that mourn in Zion, to give unto them beauty for ashes, the oil of joy for mourning, the garment of praise for the spirit of heaviness; that they might be called trees of righteousness, the planting of the LORD, that he might be glorified. (Isaiah 61:3)

I can remember getting born again in the late 1990s. I can also remember battling with thoughts of depression and despair. There were even times during that season when I contemplated suicide. Who would've thought a young man from a good family and Christian background would entertain such demonic thoughts? The truth is that there are millions of believers all over the world who battle with depression, despair, and despondency. If you do, it does not mean that you are not good enough or not strong enough. It *does* mean that the devil is eager to trap you in a prison of despair. But the good news is that there is lasting freedom in Jesus Christ. In fact, there is no place for depression in the life of a believer. We've been given the *"garment of praise for the spirit of heaviness."* Jesus said that He came to set the oppressed free and to bind up the brokenhearted. (See Luke 4:18.)

Depression is in fact a demonic spirit, but the power of God set me free from the spirit of depression. This is why I have been on a crusade for the last several years of my life to see millions of believers delivered from the insidious nature of this spirit.

Freedom is actually much simpler than people realize! The Bible says, if we will confess with our mouths and believe in our hearts that Jesus is Lord and that God raised Him from the dead, we shall be saved. (See Romans 10:9.) That word *"saved"* there also means "delivered." In other words, you and I must realize that Jesus is more powerful than depression, He is more powerful than despair, and He is way more powerful than any form of oppression that the enemy can bring our way. The moment we believe this spiritual truth is the moment that the power of depression is *broken*.

Day 35: Power Prayer

Father, in the name of Jesus, I declare that the spirit of oppression is broken off of my life completely and permanently. I declare that I no longer wear the garment of despair or the spirit of heaviness, but I have received the garment of praise instead. I declare that my future becomes brighter and brighter as I gaze into Your holy Word. I declare that the spirits of despair, hopelessness, rejection, anxiety, and fear are gone from my life. I recognize that Jesus is the Lord of my life. I also recognize that my body is the temple of the Holy Spirit, and there is no place in my thoughts, in my will, or in my emotions for any form of depression, in Jesus' name. I declare that the power of every lie of the evil one is broken off of my life right now. I will never be depressed again! I will never be bound by despair! I walk in total freedom and victory over every form of demonic oppression that the enemy would try to bring to my life. I declare these things in the matchless name of Jesus Christ. Amen!

Day 36: Purpose and Direction

And thine ears shall hear a word behind thee, saying, This is the way, walk ye in it, when ye turn to the right hand, and when ye turn to the left.   (Isaiah 30:21)

Everything in our lives revolves around purpose. In fact, it is one of the most fundamental aspects to life itself. The late Dr. Myles Munroe once said, "Where there is ignorance of purpose, abuse is inevitable." Can you imagine a person trying to eat dinner with a shovel, or attempting to change a flat tire with a fork? That would be ridiculous! Why? The items that I just mentioned were not made for that purpose. A shovel was meant for digging and a fork was meant for eating. Many people, however, are like that fork and that shovel; they are rendered useless because they're functioning outside of their purpose.

What is purpose? I love the definition in the Oxford University Press dictionary: "the reason for which something is done or created or for which something exists." What were you created to do? God is a God of divine purpose and divine direction. Direction is a course along which someone or something moves. God has a course in mind for His children. In other words, we have a divine trajectory that was charted out specifically for us by God. The more we come to know our purpose (and the One who purposed us), the more we are able to understand our trajectory—and to change it if necessary.

God does not want us ignorant of the direction that we should be walking in. He's saying to us, *"This is the way, walk ye*

it it, when ye turn to the right hand, and when ye turn to the left."
The Holy Spirit desires to guide our every footstep and lead us into the path of righteousness for His name's sake. (See Psalm 23:3.) With each new day and every moment that passes, we should be getting closer and closer to fulfilling our purpose by moving in the direction God has ordained for our lives.

Day 36: Power Prayer

Heavenly Father, I thank You for who You are and all that You have done in my life. I know that You are the Author and Finisher of my faith, and You are the Source of all knowledge, insight, and direction. As the apostle Paul declared, in You I live and move and have my being. (See Acts 17:28.) The Lord orders the steps of the righteous; therefore, I declare that You ordain my steps. I was created for the purpose of worshipping and pleasing You with every fiber of my being. Your Word declares in Proverbs 4:18 that the path of the just is like the shining light that gets brighter and brighter unto a perfect day. I declare that I walk in divine purpose. I operate with supernatural direction and insight in matters of family, ministry, and finances. I declare that I have clarity in my mind, and I am able to make the right decision every time. In the matchless name of Jesus I pray, amen!

Day 37: The Joy of the Lord

Go your way, eat the fat, and drink the sweet, and send portions unto them for whom nothing is prepared: for this day is holy unto our Lord: neither be ye sorry; for the joy of the Lord is your strength. (Nehemiah 8:10)

Contrary to popular opinion, happiness is not synonymous with joy. I have often heard Christians say, "I just want to be happy!" The truth is that happiness is relative and circumstantial, whereas joy is something much deeper. In the above verse, the Word of God declares, *"The joy of the Lord is your strength."* Paul admonishes the church in the book of Philippians, *"Rejoice in the Lord always: and again I say, Rejoice… And the peace of God, which passeth all understanding, shall keep your hearts and minds through Christ Jesus"* (Philippians 4:4, 7). In other words, rejoicing is a decision based on trusting that God will provide, as He always does. We have joy, not because of the circumstances around us, but because of God's faithfulness. You can say that joy is a revelation of the character and nature of God. This revelation strengthens and empowers the believer, because we know that He (God) will remain steadfast and consistent in all things. Through Christ Jesus, no matter what, our hearts and minds will possess the peace of God, which is beyond our understanding.

When we have joy, we can praise God in the midst of trouble. No matter what evil report comes our way, those who know their God and His Word can rejoice always. Happiness is temporary, but joy is a consequence of abiding in Christ. Joy is the fruit of our communion and fellowship with the Holy Spirit. In fact, it is not even our joy, it is *His* joy manifested in us. His joy gives us strength! The word *"strength"* comes from the Hebrew word *ma`owz*, which means "a place of safety, protection, [or] refuge." The joy of the Lord is the believer's refuge in times of trials, testing, and trouble. We can run into this shelter anytime we need to. This is what sets believers apart from people in the world. We have access to a continual stream of gladness and peace because of the Holy Spirit dwelling within us. So don't be discouraged! Don't fear! No matter what happens to you today, remember that the joy of the Lord is your strength!

Day 37: Power Prayer

Father, in the name of Jesus, I thank You for who You are and all that You have done in my life. Father, I thank You for Your goodness, which You have shown toward me. I know that You are good and Your mercy endures forever. I declare that the joy of the Lord is my strength. I declare that I possess never-ending, overflowing, abounding joy in every area of my life. I declare that my heart overflows with gladness. I declare that the revelation of Your goodness overwhelms me. I will never complain about the circumstances of my life, because You have been too good to me. I choose to rejoice in the Lord always, and in every situation, because Jesus is the Lord of the entire universe. I will never fear nor be dismayed, because Jesus Christ is the Lord of every small annoyance and every catastrophic event. I declare that the joy of the Lord is my portion in the name of Jesus. Amen!

Day 38: Holiness and Consecration

Follow peace with all men, and holiness, without which no man shall see the Lord. (Hebrews 12:14)

One of the most misunderstood and understated attributes of the Christian life is holiness. Growing up in church, I always associated holiness with the women in church who wore long dresses and head coverings. Obviously, those who dressed modestly and said spiritual things were automatically holy, right? Wrong! In fact, I discovered that true holiness really has nothing to do with the way we dress (although modesty is certainly encouraged in Scripture); instead, true holiness is reflected in the condition of our inner being.

The word *"holiness"* comes from the Greek word *hagiasmos*, which means "consecration, purification, [and] sanctification." This word carries with it the idea of being separate from sin or from the world's system. The moment we became born again, we were set apart from this world's system. The Bible tells us, *"If ye were of the world, the world would love his own: but because ye are not of the world, but I have chosen you out of the world, therefore the world hateth you"* (John 15:19). We have been chosen *out* of this world. The next time you look in the mirror, I want you to say, "I am out of this world!" Those who are children of God have been called to live a sanctified and consecrated life.

In this age of grace, sometimes it is difficult for us to fathom that God requires us to live holy lives, but this is exactly what He expects from us. Again, holiness means that God has separated us unto a divine purpose. God is separate from sin; therefore, those of us who are followers of Christ must consciously separate ourselves from anything and everything that is unclean. What entertains you? What do you listen to? Who do you surround yourself with? Holiness is the very nature of God, which manifests in us. In other words, holiness is right *being* that results in right *doing*. We have already been separated from this world in Christ; therefore, we need to sanctify ourselves in thought, word, and action.

Day 38: Power Prayer

Father, in the name of Jesus, I thank You for who You are and all that You have done in my life. I thank You for making me holy and pure in Christ. I declare that I live a sanctified life according to Your Word. I am not of this world; therefore, I choose to separate myself from the things that would defile or contaminate me. I declare that I am holy and pure on the inside, and I walk out this reality by exhibiting Christ-like behavior in every area of my life. I reject every thought, suggestion, and influence that would contaminate me or cause me to view myself outside of the confines of the Word of God. Your Word says, *"Be ye holy; for I am holy"* (1 Peter 1:16); therefore, I declare that I walk in the character and nature of God. I declare that I have been made clean on the inside. I have been set apart for a divine purpose, and I will fulfill that divine purpose in the name of Jesus. I declare that I live above this world's system and I will no longer operate in bondage in any area of my life. I declare that I am clean through the Word of God. I declare that I am morally sound and spiritually pure in the name of Jesus. Amen!

Day 39: Supernatural Favor

But the LORD was with Joseph, and shewed him mercy, and gave him favour in the sight of the keeper of the prison.
(Genesis 39:21)

Favor isn't fair!" was a phrase that I heard often in church as a young person. What does this phrase mean? Essentially, it means that whatever good thing we receive from God is not based on our own merit or goodness, but is based solely on God's faithfulness toward us. The word "*favour*" is derived from the Hebrew word *chen*, which means "grace, charm…acceptance." Even though Joseph was in prison, God's favor was upon his life. When the favor of God rest upon an individual, it doesn't matter where they find themselves; ultimately, they will see God's goodness and grace manifested in their lives. This is what it means to walk in supernatural favor. It is a divine display of God's goodness toward us that causes us to experience promotion, prosperity, and blessings. The beauty is that this favor is available to every born-again believer.

Why do we receive this favor? I am glad you asked! The Bible says, "*That the blessing of Abraham might come on the Gentiles through Jesus Christ; that we might receive the promise of the Spirit through faith*" (Galatians 3:14). Through Christ's sacrifice on the cross, the blessing of Abraham has been transferred to every single born-again believer. What does the blessing of Abraham signify? The blessing of Abraham (among other things) is the manifestation of the supernatural favor and blessing of God on our lives. Abraham walked in the favor of God all the days of his life. Everywhere he went, supernatural doors were opened to him; he experienced the prosperity and goodness of God in every area of his life, including the blessing of a child in his old age. These same blessings are available to us in Christ! The psalmist praises, *"For thou, LORD, wilt bless the righteous; with favour wilt thou compass him as with a shield"*(Psalm 5:12). Whether you recognize it or not, you are surrounded with a supernatural crown (shield) of favor. It is time for you to walk in the favor of God!

Day 39: Power Prayer

Father, I thank You for who You are and all that You have done in my life. I declare that I am a seed of Abraham and the blessing of Abraham is upon my life. I walk in Your supernatural favor and blessing in every area of my life. Supernatural doors are opened to me. I declare that I walk in prosperity, increase, and abundance in every area of life. People are compelled to do good things for me because Your hand of blessing and favor is upon my life. I declare that the favor of the Lord surrounds me as a shield, keeping the blessings of God *in* and everything contrary to the blessing *out*. I receive divine promotion, prosperity, contracts, debt cancellation, divine opportunities, and supernatural wisdom right now. Just as Joseph found favor in the keeper of the prison, I declare that I have found favor in the sight of all those around me, including my boss, family members, pastor, supervisors, constituents, neighbors, children, and any other person that has been placed in my life by God. I declare that something good is going to happen in my life today, because of the supernatural favor upon my life, in the name of Jesus. Amen!

Day 40: Divine Wisdom

Wisdom is the principal thing; therefore get wisdom: and with all thy getting get understanding.

(Proverbs 4:7)

Wisdom is highly prized in the Bible—especially in the book of Proverbs. But what is wisdom? When the Bible talks about wisdom, it's talking about the right application of knowledge. It is talking about the capacity to make right decisions according to the Word of God. The truth is, we need wisdom in order to prosper and succeed in every area of our lives. Wisdom helps us understand the purpose of a thing. When we know the purpose of the thing we can interact with that thing the right way, and so wisdom is absolutely essential.

What does wisdom look like? James tells us clearly: *"But the wisdom that is from above is first pure, then peaceable, gentle, and easy to be intreated, full of mercy and good fruits, without partiality, and without hypocrisy"* (James 3:17). Can you imagine your knowledge being clothed with these incredible attributes, and becoming the beautiful wisdom from above? Well, God desires for you to have this wisdom, so that you can function in your assignment! James also lets us know that if we don't have wisdom we should ask for it: *"If any of you lack wisdom, let him ask of God, that giveth to all men liberally, and upbraideth not; and it shall be given him"* (James 1:5). Prayer, then, is the mechanism through which God imparts purpose and direction in our lives, giving us His wisdom.

The more we pray in faith, the more we are conscious of who we are and the direction God wants us to walk in. Have you ever needed wisdom for a major decision in your life? What did you do? Most people simply try to figure out what they should do rather than ask God, who is willing to give us wisdom freely. I believe that God wants to reveal your purpose and give you strategic direction in the affairs of your life. The wisdom you're searching for is only one prayer away!

Day 40: Power Prayer

Father, I thank You for the power of Your Word. I recognize that You are the Source for all divine wisdom. Your Word declares that wisdom is the principal thing, and so we should get wisdom, and in all our getting, get understanding. I recognize that Your wisdom is infinite; it expands to the deep recesses of the universe. You know all things, and all knowledge comes from You. I know that Your Word is the source for all wisdom and knowledge. I declare that I walk in supernatural wisdom in every area of my life, and I declare that I am not deficient in any area of my life. Today, I applied my heart to receive wisdom, understanding, and knowledge. I declare that I make right decisions according to Your Word. I received an impartation of Your wisdom right now! Because I am receptive to Your voice and obedient to Your Word, I can never be led astray by the enemy. Thank You, Lord, for the manifestation of Your divine wisdom in my life. In the name of Jesus, amen!

123

Day 41: Total Turnaround

And the LORD turned the captivity of Job, when he prayed for his friends: also the LORD gave Job twice as much as he had before. (Job 42:10)

Have you ever felt stagnant or stuck in your life? I don't know about you, but I have been through some very dark seasons. There have been times where I felt like my life was going in the wrong direction. I travel often, and as such, I have become accustomed to using a GPS. Most GPS devices have the ability to tell you your current location and also direct you to where you want to go. On one occasion, I was following my GPS system and I made a wrong turn. I then noticed that my GPS recalculated my route and said, "In 100 feet, make a U-turn!"

Many people are in need of a similar turnaround in their spiritual lives. Maybe the enemy has caused you to lose focus or move in the wrong direction. Maybe you feel like your life is absolutely out of control. Maybe you are noticing increased temptation because of a situation you are in or people you are with. Maybe you are a perfect candidate for a total turnaround! If so, you can identify with Job.

Job lost everything that he deemed valuable. His children died unexpectedly, sickness ravished his body, and his wife dismissed him. This was a terrible situation! However, God had a greater plan. God has a way of turning your mess into a message, and your misery into ministry! In the case of Job, the Bible records: *"And the LORD turned the captivity of Job, when he prayed for his friends: also the LORD gave Job twice as much as he had before"* (Job 42:10). The word *"turned"* in this passage means "to turn back or restore." Job was headed in one direction physically, spiritually, and emotionally but God recalculated his route through *His* GPS (God's Positioning System) and turned him around onto a path of blessings, favor, and prosperity. Job received double for his trouble! I believe God wants to do the same thing in your life. If your life is not headed in the right direction, now is the time to receive a *total turnaround* in the name of Jesus.

Day 41: Power Prayer

Father, in the name of Jesus, I thank You for Your faithfulness toward me. Your goodness reaches to the heavens, and Your mercy endures forever. Your Word declares in Jeremiah 29:11, *"For I know the thoughts that I think toward you, saith the Lord, thoughts of peace, and not of evil, to give you an expected end."* I declare that Your plans for me, and thoughts toward me, are good. I declare that every obstacle that stands before me is removed, and all spiritual resistance is neutralized. I declare that today is my day of total turnaround. I declare that I shall receive double for my trouble! Lord, I thank You in advance for turning my captivity into rejoicing and releasing supernatural breakthrough in my life. I declare that I shall recover everything that the enemy has taken from me, including my dignity and peace of mind. I declare that I shall be one thousand times greater today than I was yesterday. I declare that the blessings of the Lord pursue me and overtake me in every area of my life. I declare that I receive divine multiplication and increase in my life. Today is my day of total and complete turnaround! Today is my day of supernatural prosperity and breakthrough in the name of Jesus! Amen!

Day 42: All Things Working For Good

And we know that all things work together for good to them that love God, to them who are the called according to his purpose. (Romans 8:28)

Have you ever attended a symphony orchestra? I have always been fascinated by the skill and ability of the symphony conductor to take all of the different instruments and arrange them into beautiful melodic sounds. How is this even possible? Because of the phenomenon of harmony, separate instruments can blend, and sway, and complement each other in a seemingly effortless display.

Well, God is the master orchestrator of our lives! He, in His infinite wisdom and power, knows how to take the seemingly chaotic things in our lives and produce the most beautiful and harmonious sounds. This is what the Bible was referring to in Romans 8:28, when it says, *"And we know that all things work together for good to them that love God, to them who are the called according to his purpose."* As prophetic intercessors, we have the unique ability to look at trials, tests, and difficulties from a heavenly perspective. Instead of viewing the situations in your life as problems, view them as chords, which, however dissonant or wrong-sounding, can be used by God to create a beautiful song. The key to seeing this divine symphony come to fruition is prayer. Paul was speaking in the context of intercession when he wrote, *"All things work together..."* Too many believers are not engaging in prayer, and therefore find it difficult to see the symphony that God desires to orchestrate. Pray with all of your heart, and allow God to create a beautiful song.

Day 42: Power Prayer

Father, in the name of Jesus, I thank You for Your goodness and grace toward me. I declare that all things work together for my good, because I love You, Lord, and I am called according to Your divine purpose. I declare that my life is a divine symphony of Your grace. I declare that I am in the center of Your will. You are the divine arranger and orchestrator of my destiny; therefore, I declare that all is well with every area of my life. I know that You work all things after the counsel of Your will. Your Word is Your will; therefore, I declare that everything in my life is working according to Your holy Word. I will never be afraid, angry, or frustrated about my future because I recognize that You are in control. Today, I declare that the goodness and favor of God abounds toward me. Every situation, circumstance, and trial in my life is simply a chord in the divine orchestration of my destiny; therefore, I rejoice in You always! I have peace and tranquility because I recognize that You are infinitely wise and omni-benevolent (all good). Thank You, Lord, for working in my life. I declare that whatever the enemy meant for evil has already been turned around for my good and for the glory of God! Amen!

128

Day 43: Seeing the Unseen

*By faith he forsook Egypt, not fearing the wrath of the king:
for he endured, **as seeing him who is invisible**.*

(Hebrews 11:27)

heard a story once about a class of young people who were participating in an earth science experiment. Their teacher wanted the students to explore the vast world of microorganisms around them, and so he took the students to a nearby pond and told them to collect some water into a petri dish. Then he asked them what they saw. Most of the students laughed and said that they saw nothing in the dish except water. Once all the students collected their water samples, he took them to the science lab where they placed the dishes under a microscope. To their amazement, the students discovered that the water was *teeming* with living microorganisms.

In many ways, this science experiment accurately reflects the spiritual realm. Most people are unaware that the spiritual realm is of a deeper and truer reality than the physical realm. In other words, the unseen world is more real than the seen world. Just as the students thought that there was nothing but water in the dish because that's all they could see, so many believers have been locked into a physical perspective. What changed the student's perspective? A microscope! Once they looked at the water with a microscope, their eyes were opened to the unseen realm. The Bible tells us that the things in the created world were not made of things that are seen, but of things that are unseen. (See Hebrews 11:3.)

God wants to open your spiritual eyes to gaze upon the magnificent reality of the unseen realm. In the natural world, you may feel all alone, but in the realm of the spirit, you are surrounded with an entire host of warring angels. Hallelujah! God has already blessed you with all spiritual blessings in the heavenly realm; you simply need to open your spiritual eyes. Just as Moses saw Him who was invisible, God desires to open your eyes to the invisible realm. Prayer is the key!

Day 43: Power Prayer

Father, in the name of Jesus Christ, I thank You for the truth and power of Your Word. I declare that my spiritual eyes are opened to the unseen realm, the realm of the Spirit, and I declare that what is in the unseen realm is of a deeper and truer reality than the physical world. I declare that I am unmoved by the physical realm (i.e. sight, touch, sound), but Your Word is the only thing that moves me. I declare that the Word of God is the final authority in my life. I choose to believe the report of the Lord above any other report. I declare that the promises of God are real and tangible in my life. I declare that I am blessed with all spiritual blessings in heavenly places, in Christ. I am prosperous! I am anointed! I am well-favored, because I have Christ inside! I declare that I (and my loved ones) are already healed, delivered, and set free by the blood of Jesus. I declare that I was already healed and restored two thousand years ago, through the cross of Jesus Christ. My spiritual eyes are open and keen to the reality of heaven, angels, and spiritual warfare. I recognize that I do not wrestle against flesh and blood, but against unseen forces in the spiritual realm. I stand victorious in Christ. I declare that I have eyes to see and ears to hear in Jesus' name! Amen!

131

Day 44: Divine Revelation

*But as it is written, Eye hath not seen, nor ear heard, neither have entered into the heart of man, the things which God hath prepared for them that love him. But **God hath revealed them unto us by his Spirit:** for the Spirit searcheth all things, yea, the deep things of God.*

(1 Corinthians 2:9–10)

One of my favorite holidays growing up was Christmas. Unfortunately, this had nothing to do with the deep significance of celebrating the birth of Christ into the world. No, Christmas was my favorite holiday for one reason and one reason alone: presents! I can remember one Christmas in particular that I was so excited, I was not able to sleep the night before. Early in the morning, I ran downstairs and began to unwrap my gifts that I had been staring at, but unable to touch until Christmas morning. And when I eagerly ripped off the wrapping paper, I saw the actual presents that I had been blessed with.

You could say that the gifts were *unveiled*. They were already under the tree, but they were concealed behind wrapping paper. This is the same idea as the biblical term "revelation," or, in Greek, *apokaluptō*, which means "to uncover, lay open what has been veiled or covered up." As New Testament believers, God wants to reveal the mysteries of His will to us. One day when I was driving in my car, I heard the Holy Spirit ask me a profound question: "Kynan, what is revelation?" I answered with the best theological answer I could muster: "To unveil something that was once hidden!" Then the Holy Spirit asked me a follow-up question. "How do you know when you have received a revelation?" Honestly, I couldn't really answer this question. In my silence, I heard the Holy Spirit respond for me, "When everything changes!"

Contrary to popular belief, revelation is not the same as information. Many people receive great information about God every Sunday, but they still live the same way after they leave. What is the problem? They haven't received revelation. Revelation brings something that was hidden into manifestation in our lives, with the result of literally, actually changing us. The Holy Spirit wants to give us a revelation of the Word of God (and the promises of God) that will transform our lives. True revelation always brings transformation. God wants to "unwrap" the hidden gifts and treasures that He has placed inside us. Many believers are ignorant of the things that God has prepared for them; they need a revelation! Prayer postures our heart to receive that revelation. The more we pray, the more God will reveal to us.

133

Day 44: Power Prayer

Father, in the name of Jesus Christ, I thank You for the unfailing power of Your Word. I know that it is Your desire to reveal Your blessings, gifts, and promises to me. I declare that I walk in divine revelation in every area of my life! I declare that the things in my life that need to be unveiled are revealed right now! I declare that my spirit is receptive to the revelation of the Holy Spirit. As I apply my heart to understanding, I thank You for manifesting Your truth within me. I receive revelation concerning the affairs of my life. Holy Spirit, I ask You to speak to me right now! Reveal to me the things that I need to know. I receive divine revelation for my finances, career, ministry, health, family, children, and future. Prayer is the catalyst for divine revelation; therefore, I declare that nothing will take me by surprise because I am a praying person. I declare that my spiritual eyes and ears are open to what You desire to reveal to me. I declare that my life will never be the same again! Amen!

Day 45: More than Conquerors

Nay, in all these things we are more than conquerors through him that loved us.   (Romans 8:37)

Too many believers are investing their time, energy, and resources on survival. What do I mean? There are millions of Christians all over the world who are barely getting by. They just want to make it to heaven, yet they are being tormented by the enemy while down here on earth. I do not believe this is the will of God. I believe that God has called us to walk victoriously on this side of heaven. This is why Paul the apostle exclaimed, *"Nay, in all these things we are more than conquerors through him that loved us."* No matter what we go through or face in this life, it is important for us to know that we are more than conquerors!

What does that mean? The phrase *"more than conquerors"* is a Greek term that denotes gaining "a surpassing victory." In other words, we aren't to just barely get by, but we are to walk in surpassing victory because the enemy of our souls is a defeated foe. You heard me right! The enemy you face has already undergone a humiliating defeat. Simply put, you are fighting a loser! Many Christians don't recognize that Satan has already lost, so they succumb to his lies and intimidating tactics; but when you understand that the battle has already been won on your behalf, then you can stand in a posture of confidence and victory.

Today, I challenge you to recognize who you are and what Christ has already done for you. Know that if God is for you, who can be against you? (See Romans 8:31.) God does not want you to be miserable on earth. He does not want you to be depressed, oppressed, and defeated; rather, He desires for you to enjoy the abundant life and walk in complete freedom and victory.

Day 45: Power Prayer

Father, in the name of Jesus Christ of Nazareth, I thank You for the finished work of the cross. I declare that I am more than a conqueror through the One who loves me unconditionally. I declare that I walk in total freedom and victory in my life! I refuse to submit to the intimidation and lies of the evil one; instead, I declare that I am strong, bold, and victorious in Christ. There is no tactic of the evil one that can be effective against me because I am full of the Holy Spirit and power. I prophesy to every situation and circumstance in my life, and I say, "Greater is He who lives in me than he that is in the world!" I declare that all confusion, fear, and defeat must go from me right now! I declare that I will never be defeated, depressed, or despondent again. I forbid the activity of the devil in my life today! I declare that the devil picked a fight with the wrong born-again believer; he must flee from me right now in the name of Jesus! Amen!

136

Day 46: Will You Be Made Whole?

When Jesus saw him lie [down], and knew that he had been now a long time in that case, he saith unto him, Wilt thou be made whole?   (John 5:6)

In my many years of supernatural ministry, I have come across countless people who did not realize (for one reason or another) that it was the unconditional will of God to heal them. In fact, I remember talking to a woman who said that her anxiety attacks were a gift of God to teach her to appreciate life. This is absurd! And there are still many others who believe it is God's will to heal or deliver them, but they have relegated this deliverance to some future time. This is what I call "God will later syndrome."

There was a character in the Gospels who suffered from this very thing. He was incapacitated for thirty-eight years, and he was waiting for the opportunity to enter into the Pool of Bethesda in order to receive his long-awaited miracle. The problem was that every time he attempted to enter the waters, someone else went in ahead of him. Fortunately, Jesus showed up on the scene, and whenever Jesus shows up, the impossible becomes possible. Jesus asked this man a profound question, "Will you be made whole?" You would think this gentleman would have answered with a resounding "Yes, Lord!" Instead, he made excuses for his condition.

Doesn't this sound so familiar? People tend to make excuses when they feel discouraged about the circumstances of their lives. The man at the pool didn't realize that Jesus was greater than the Pool of Bethesda. Jesus was healing, deliverance, and restoration incarnate. After listening to the man, Jesus simply says, "Arise, take up your bed, and walk." (See John 5:8.) These three simple commands radically changed the man's life forever. What is that you are waiting on today? Is it healing? Is it restoration? God is asking you the same question as the man at the pool, "Will you be made whole?" The time for excuses has expired and the time for deliverance is now!

Day 46: Power Prayer

Father, in the name of Jesus Christ, I thank You for who You are and all that You have done in my life. I thank You, Lord, that it is Your unconditional will to heal and deliver me in every area of my life. I declare that Your power surpasses any physical, spiritual, mental, or emotional limitation I face in my life. I declare that I am made whole by the power of Your love. I refuse to accept or tolerate any excuses. I declare that Your Word is the final authority in my life. I will not allow the enemy to bully, intimidate, or bind me again. I speak to every crippled area in my life and/or the lives of my loved ones and I say, "Arise, take up your bed, and walk!" I choose to walk in the fullness of the power of God and not rely on my own abilities. Today is my day of miracles! Today is my day of breakthrough! I declare that my family, finances, godly relationships, and physical health are made whole in the name of Jesus! I declare that I am restored and walk in total restoration in the name of Jesus. Amen!

Day 47: Blessed and Broken

And he commanded the multitude to sit down on the grass,
and took the five loaves, and the two fishes, and looking up
to heaven, he blessed, and brake, and gave the loaves to his
disciples, and the disciples to the multitude.

(Matthew 14:19)

One of the most powerful principles that I have ever learned is the principle of divine multiplication. I often refer to this in other writings as the "Law of Multiplication." One New Year's Eve, our church held a special prayer and worship service. At this time we were a very small church and were not expecting a large crowd, so we only bought a small quantity of food to share with our guests after the event. To our surprise, we had the largest attendance yet! We were excited about the attendance, but a little frantic—what were we going to do about the food? Honestly, we were so caught up in the worship that we actually forgot about the food shortage. With only enough food to feed a few people, we blessed it and gave it to our guests. To our amazement, the food literally multiplied. Not only did we feed a multitude, but also we actually had leftovers for an entire week.

Our experience, of course, reminded me of the miraculous feeding of the crowd in the book of Matthew. The disciples realized that the multitudes had no food, and they anxiously reported this food crisis to Jesus. All they had was two fish and five loaves of bread (which was enough food for a small boy). The disciples must have been surprised by what they heard next: *"Give ye them to eat."* Maybe Jesus didn't hear what they said—or maybe there was a miracle in the works. The Bible says that He took the loaves and He blessed them and broke them.

The first key to experiencing divine multiplication is the blessing. This is the word *eulogeō*, which means "to consecrate a thing with solemn prayers." If you want something to multiply in your life, you must first consecrate it with prayer. Next was the breaking. The word "break" simply means to separate in pieces. It represents sanctification. In the kingdom of God, whatever we consecrate in prayer and separate for God's purpose, we give permission to multiply! God wants you to experience multiplication in your life. Are you ready to be blessed? Are you willing to be broken?

141

Day 47: Power Prayer

Father, in the name of Jesus Christ, I thank You for Your Word. I know that it is Your will for me to experience supernatural multiplication in every area of my life. I declare that every portion of my life is blessed. I declare that everything in my life is sanctified for Your divine purposes. I declare that You have the power to take the scarce things in my life and use them to feed multitudes. Your Word declares that You prepare a table before me in the presence of my enemies. I declare that You are the good Shepherd, who gives His life for the sheep. I declare that I walk in supernatural abundance. I declare that all grace abounds toward me! I will never lack anything, because the Lord is my Shepherd and I shall not want. (See Psalm 23:1.) I declare that Your goodness and grace abound toward me, and that I, having all sufficiency in all things, abound to every good work in the name of Jesus. Amen!

142

Day 48: The Power of Forgiveness

Forbearing one another, and forgiving one another, if any man have a quarrel against any: even as Christ forgave you, so also do ye. (Colossians 3:13)

Growing up in a fairly large family, offenses were a regular part of my childhood. I was no stranger to harsh words or even (at times) bullying. However, we were taught as a family not to fight and quarrel, and if there was a dispute, we were encouraged to forgive one another. As members of the family of God, we must adopt the same philosophy. What is forgiveness and why is it so important? Forgiveness is a function of love. By nature, love keeps no record of wrong. (See 1 Corinthians 13.) In the book of Colossians, Paul admonishes the church: *"Forbearing one another, and forgiving one another, if any man have a quarrel against any: even as Christ forgave you, so also do ye."* The word *"forgiving"* here means "to show oneself gracious [or]…to pardon." Essentially, to forgive is to release someone from their debt. It means to pardon another person's trespasses toward you.

Of course, this is exactly what God did through the cross of Christ; He pardoned our sins eternally, and released us from the guilt and condemnation that ruled our hearts. How can we say that we are believers in Jesus Christ and refuse to release our brothers or sisters who offend us? The thing about forgiveness is that it has no boundaries, stipulations, or expiration dates.

Christ did not ask us how many sins we committed or how long ago we sinned; He simply forgave us on the basis of His sacrifice on the cross. This doesn't mean that we are to *accept* all behavior, or *restore relationships* with everyone who has hurt us, but it does mean that we are commanded by God to release all offenses in our heart.

The Scripture says, *"But if ye do not forgive, neither will your Father which is in heaven forgive your trespasses"* (Mark 11:26). Harboring offense and refusing to forgive is hazardous to our spiritual health as well as our physical health. Too many believers are spiritually, physically, and emotionally sick because of a refusal to release the hurts and offenses they have endured. It doesn't matter what was done to you or how painful it was, you must make a decision today to walk in forgiveness. Your peace of mind, health, and freedom depend on it!

144

Day 48: Power Prayer

Father, in the name of Jesus, I thank You for Your great love toward me. Thank You for sending Your Son, Jesus Christ, to die on the cross for my sins, and thereby forgiving me of all my sins and cleansing me from all iniquity. I declare that Your Word is the final authority in my life. I make a conscious decision (as an act of my free will) to freely and completely forgive all others as I would have You to forgive me. I ask that You forgive me for holding on to grudges, harboring offenses, or allowing bitterness to take root in my heart. I release all debtors. I forgive all those who have hurt me (especially authority figures) and I declare that the legal right that the enemy had to my peace of mind as a result of offense has been annulled. I declare that I am completely free from all hurts, disappointments, and offenses. I declare that the peace and restoration of God flood my soul right now in the name of Jesus. Amen!

Day 49: Free Indeed!

If the Son therefore shall make you free, ye shall be free indeed. (John 8:36)

Years ago, I had a friend who spent a significant time in prison. After being released, he went back to the same criminal activity that had landed him in prison the first time. Even though he had been released physically, he was still a prisoner psychologically and emotionally. He wasn't truly free!

What does it mean to be free? What does lasting freedom look like? In the gospel of John, Jesus declared: *"If the Son therefore shall make you free, ye shall be free indeed."* I love the word *"free"* in this passage; it literally means "set at liberty from the dominion of sin." Before Christ, sin ruled and dominated us. Even when we wanted to do what was right, we found ourselves incapable of following through. Why? Because we were slaves! In a preceding verse, Jesus said, *"Whosoever committeth sin is the servant* [slave] *of sin"* (John 8:34). It is the will of God for all His children to enjoy true and lasting freedom in every area of their lives.

Maybe you or someone you know has struggled with an area of bondage. Maybe you have wrestled with addictions. No matter how difficult or long-lasting your struggle, you can be free today! In other words, you can be *"free indeed."* This comes from the Greek word *ontōs*, which means "truly, in reality, in point of fact, as opposed to what is fictitious, pretended, [or] false." In other words, God doesn't want you pretending to be free in front of others but still bound on the inside. It is like a person saying that they are free from nicotine addiction while still smoking a couple packs a day. The devil is a liar! That is not the freedom Christ came to give us. Real freedom is the power and ability to reject what once had you bound. We have been made free by the blood of the Lamb. The moment we accept this truth, the moment we will begin to experience the kind of freedom the Word of God promises. All you have to do is call on the name of the Lord with a pure heart, and He will make you free today.

Day 49: Power Prayer

Father, in the name of Jesus, I thank You for who You are and all that You have done in my life. I thank You for the power of Your blood! Your Word declares that if the Son shall make you free, you will be free indeed. Right now, I expose my entire spirit, soul, and body to the Word of God, to the blood of Jesus Christ, and to the fire of the Holy Spirit. I command anything operating in my life that was not planted by You to be uprooted right now. Devil, I loose myself from you in the name of Jesus. I command you and all of your demons to go from me right now. I declare that I am made free by the blood of the Lamb, and by the power of the Holy Spirit. I declare that I am truly free in all areas of my life. Sin and bondage now no longer have a right to operate in my life. I declare that I am 100 percent free in the name of Jesus. Amen!

Day 50: No Weapon Formed

> *No weapon that is formed against thee shall prosper; and every tongue that shall rise against thee in judgment thou shalt condemn. This is the heritage of the servants of the LORD, and their righteousness is of me, saith the LORD.* (Isaiah 54:17)

Many years ago, I worked in the insurance business. I would sell life and health insurance policies to those in need of coverage. A policy is simply a legal document outlining the benefits of the insured and the responsibilities of the insurer. Most customers rarely read their policy, and this is why they are often taken by surprise when they file a claim.

The Word of God is like that insurance policy. In it, we are promised certain benefits and blessings. One of these benefits is divine protection against the slanderous tongue. As I mentioned previously, words are very powerful. They have the power to build up and tear down. The devil is the accuser of the brethren, and he makes it his business to launch verbal accusations, slanders, and curses at God's people. Little does the enemy of our soul know that we have coverage against curses and slander in our "policy": *"No weapon that is formed against thee shall prosper; and every tongue that shall rise against thee in judgment thou shalt condemn."* I call this the Isaiah 54:17 coverage.

Notice that it never promised us that weapons wouldn't form, but it does promise that when they are formed, they will not prosper (or succeed). The Bible goes further to say that every tongue that rises against us in judgment, we shall condemn. This is the Hebrew word *rasha*, which means "to condemn as guilty (in civil relations)." Don't be dismayed by the lies and accusations that are being launched against you. You are covered! Every false accusation leveled against you will come under condemnation. Unfortunately, I am speaking from experience! I have learned to stand on the Word of God and watch Him enforce His promises.

Day 50: Power Prayer

Father, in the name of Jesus, I thank You for the promises of Your holy Word. I know that Your Word will never return void, but will accomplish everything that You have sent it to do. I declare that Your Word is the final authority in my life. I declare that no weapon formed against me will prosper, and every false accusation, slander, lie, or curse spoken by the evil one, and those under his influence, will be condemned. I declare that the blood of Jesus covers me, and I dwell under the shadow of His wings. I declare that no evil thing will be able to take root in my life. I say "return to sender" to every curse spoken against me or my loved ones in the name of Jesus. I declare that anyone being used by the devil to speak evil against me is released from their demonic assignment right now, and is set free by the power of the blood. I declare that all assaults from the evil one will cease and desist right now, in the name of Jesus. I declare the divine enforcement of every promise in the Word of God for my life. I declare that it is well with every area of my life in the name of Jesus. Amen!

Day 51: The Tongue of the Learned

The Lord God hath given me the tongue of the learned, that I should know how to speak a word in season to him that is weary: he wakeneth morning by morning, he wakeneth mine ear to hear as the learned.   (Isaiah 50:4)

As a pastor, I have had my share of verbal blunders. I have said things that I should not have said, and at times, not known what to say when I should have said something. Have you ever been in that place? The truth is that words are very powerful. They have the ability to shape our destinies. The Bible says, *"The mouth of the righteous speaketh wisdom, and his tongue talketh of judgment"* (Psalm 37:30). The right words at the right time can have a profound impact on the circumstances of your life. They can make or break a promotion or other opportunity. Our words can bring consolation and comfort to those in despair. The more I began to realize this truth, the more I began to pray about speaking the right things.

As prophetic people, our words are even more impactful, because of the supernatural power they carry. One day I read this powerful Scripture, and it changed my life: *"The Lord God hath given me the tongue of the learned, that I should know how to speak"* (Isaiah 50:4). Isaiah prayed to Jehovah that He would give him the tongue of the learned. What does this mean? It means a taught or discipled tongue. Has your tongue been discipled? Too many believers have no control over their tongue, and, as a result, their lives are chaotic. Notice also the *reason* why we ought to have a learned tongue: to give a word of comfort at the right time. Have you ever needed to hear a word from God at a particular time in your life? How refreshing was it to hear someone speak to your specific situation when you needed encouragement? This prophetic skill is available to every single believer! All you have to do is ask!

Day 51: Power Prayer

Father, in the name of Jesus, I thank You for the truth and power of Your Word. Thank You for Your grace and mercy! I declare that I possess the tongue of the learned, and I am equipped to speak a word in season to those who need to hear Your voice. I declare that my ears are awakened to hear as the learned. I declare that my tongue is under divine control. I declare that my tongue has a prophetic assignment and responsibility to only speak those things that are pleasing to Your ear. I declare that I possess a gracious tongue; my mouth is full of edification, exhortation, comfort, and consolation. I declare that people are benefited by the wisdom that resides in my heart and mouth. I declare that my mouth is a divine orifice of supernatural power and I only speak things that align with the unadulterated Word of God. I will never be afraid of speaking the wrong things, as my tongue has been redeemed from a cursed nature. I declare that my spirit is awakened to the power of Your Word in the name of Jesus. Amen!

Day 52: Know the Truth

And ye shall know the truth, and the truth shall make you free. (John 8:32)

I have heard it said (on more than one occasion) that the truth shall make you free. But that statement is incomplete! Contrary to popular belief, it is not the truth you *hear* that makes you free. The Bible says, "And ye shall **know** the truth, and the truth shall make you free." The Scripture essentially says that it is not the truth alone that makes you free, but knowledge of the truth.

The word *"know"* comes from the Greek word *ginōskō*, which means "to know, understand, [or] perceive." It is rooted in a Jewish idiomatic expression for sexual intercourse. *"And Adam knew Eve his wife; and she conceived, and bare Cain, and said, I have gotten a man from the LORD"* (Genesis 4:1). This kind of knowing is so much more than just mental assent. To *know* the truth means to have a deep and intimate understanding of the truth.

Why is this so significant? Because the truth is so much more than an idea; the truth is a Person! Jesus said, *"I am the way, the truth, and the life: no man cometh unto the Father, but by me"* (John 14:6). The more we know the truth, the more freedom we will see manifested in our lives. Before I knew the truth about healing, I accepted sickness in my life as an option; however, when I came to know Jesus as the Healer, I could no longer tolerate sickness and disease. This is the difference between head knowledge and deep revelation. When you know something, you know it! The devil cannot talk you out of the truth that you know. The key to lasting freedom in our lives is the knowledge of the truth. The moment the truth is revealed (and known), the power of the lie is broken. Every area of bondage in a believer's life is connected (in some way) to a lie they have believed. Break the lie, reveal the truth, and watch the freedom manifest itself!

Day 52: Power Prayer

Father, I thank You for Your omnipotent power and grace. I thank You for the truth of Your Word. Jesus is the living truth, the living Word. I declare that the unadulterated truth of the Word of God has the power to make me free. I declare that I am free because I know the truth about who You are and who I am. Jesus, You are the way, the truth and the life; no one can come to the Father but through You. I declare that You have already made me free from the power of sin through the cross. I declare that freedom, deliverance, and breakthrough are my portion. Every area of my life is renewed through the power of the Word of God. I declare that my loved ones are liberated from the powers of darkness through the truth of Your Word. I declare that my inner being has a revelation of God's Word; therefore, I can never be bound by the lies of the enemy again, in the name of Jesus. Amen!

Day 53: Dispelling the Darkness

For we wrestle not against flesh and blood, but against principalities, against powers, against the rulers of the darkness of this world, against spiritual wickedness in high places. (Ephesians 6:12)

As a young, newly saved believer, I was completely ignorant of spiritual warfare. The only thing I knew about the devil was that it was best to stay away from him. I figured that if I stayed away from him, he would stay away from me. I was absolutely wrong! In fact, I discovered that it is the responsibility of the believer to *dispel* the darkness in their lives. Let me be clear, I am not saying it is our responsibility to defeat the enemy; Jesus took care of that on the cross. However, we *have* been given spiritual weapons for the purpose of enforcing the devil's defeat and dismantling his influence in our lives and the lives of our loved ones. Every time we pray for our loved ones, we are breaking the power of the enemy's influence in their lives. Hallelujah! We need not be afraid of any spiritual backlash or retaliation; the blood of Jesus covers us.

One night, while nearly being suffocated in my sleep by a spirit of oppression, I literally screamed out, "Jesus!" The darkness lifted, and I had an epiphany: the name of Jesus was more powerful than the darkness. No matter what the enemy is attempting to do in your life, you must understand that the devil has no power over you. The only power the enemy possesses is in the lies that you believe. The first step to dispelling the darkness in your life or the lives of your loved ones is to believe the truth. Once we believe the truth and speak the truth, we cripple all demonic activity in our lives. As prophetic people, you have been called by God to push back the darkness in every sphere of influence in your life. You can push back the darkness in your family, home, school, job, and community. Tell the devil, "No more!" Let him know that you will no longer accept or tolerate his activity in your life, because you are a child of the Most High God!

Day 53: Power Prayer

Father, in the name of Jesus Christ of Nazareth, I declare that Your Word is full of supernatural power. Your Word says that we do not wrestle against flesh and blood, but against principalities, powers, and the rulers of the darkness of this world; therefore, I declare that all powers of darkness are broken off my life. I declare that all spiritual darkness must flee from me right now. I declare that the blood of the Lamb, Jesus, covers my family. I declare that no weapon formed against me shall prosper. I declare that anxiety and fear have no more place in my life. I declare that all oppression, depression, and all spiritual attacks must leave me now, in the name of Jesus. I am not afraid of the dark, neither spiritually nor physically. I declare that I am victorious in spiritual battle. I declare that all ignorance and misinformation are removed from my thought life right now. I declare that I stand in total victory in the name of Jesus. Amen!

157

Day 54: Spiritual Awakening

And it shall come to pass in the last days, saith God, I will pour out of my Spirit upon all flesh: and your sons and your daughters shall prophesy, and your young men shall see visions, and your old men shall dream dreams: and on my servants and on my handmaidens I will pour out in those days of my Spirit; and they shall prophesy.

(Acts 2:17–18)

In mid-1700s, there was a great spiritual awakening in America. And again in the 1900s, there was a powerful outpouring of the Holy Spirit in America. I believe that we are on the cusp of a third great awakening in our country and in the world. The truth is that awakening does not take place in a vacuum, but is the result of earnest men and women seeking God with all of their hearts. I believe that the awakening that we are looking for has already begun. It has begun in our hearts! The dissatisfaction that you feel with "church as usual" is actually from God. God has a way of using discontentment to stir people to action.

The Bible tells us, in the book of Joel, that the Lord would pour out His Spirit on the last days. (See Joel 2:28.) Contrary to popular belief, this is not some spiritual phenomenon that will take place in the distant future. In fact, this outpouring began two thousand years ago. It was Peter, quoting from the book of Joel, who said that the baptism of the Holy Spirit, with the accompanying evidence of speaking in tongues, was a fulfillment of the prophecy given by the prophet Joel. In other words, revival has already begun. God is waiting on you! Revival takes place when the revived people take action! You are the revival that this nation is looking for. You are the revival that your community needs. Why? Because you are a carrier of the Holy Spirit, the same Spirit who raised Jesus from the dead. What are you waiting for? Spread the fire!

Day 54: Power Prayer

Father, in the name of Jesus Christ, I thank You for who You are and all that You have done in my life. I know that Your Word created the physical universe. I know that Your Word will never return void. Paul said that Your Word was the power that produces salvation; therefore, I declare that the power of Your Word is made manifest in and through my life. I declare that I am a prophetic revivalist. The spirit of revival rests upon me! I declare that I am an agent of change. I release Your supernatural power for revival and awakening right now. I declare that my church is a church of revival. I declare that the Holy Spirit revives my home. I declare that my heart burns with heaven's agenda. I declare that a great awakening will soon shake the nations. The nations will be transformed by the power of God's love. I declare that the world will be turned upside down once again by the revelation of Jesus Christ. Amen!

159

Day 55: Developing Spiritual Hunger

Blessed are they which do hunger and thirst after righteousness: for they shall be filled. (Matthew 5:6)

What does it mean to be hungry? Have you ever truly been hungry? On my first mission trip to Haiti, I saw real hunger firsthand. There were three-year-old children who had not eaten for three days. We fed over four hundred children during that particular trip. Some of the missionaries were concerned that the children would not be able to eat such large quantities of beef and rice, but to their surprise, the children devoured the food. They were literally starving!

Jesus said, *"Blessed are they which do hunger and thirst after righteousness: for they shall be filled."* The word *"hunger"* here means to crave or desire ardently. In the Western world, most people have not seen real hunger (although there are certainly exceptions, starvation isn't the norm). In fact, we often eat so much junk food that we have not allowed our bodies to experience real hunger. Most times our bodies have not even had the opportunity to detoxify before we fill our stomachs with more.

Well, the same has been true of the church. Many have been consuming so much spiritual junk food that they have not had the opportunity to develop a hunger for the things of God. How do you know when you're hungry? When a man is hungry, he will make sacrifices. Hunger causes you to forget about the opinions of men. Thirst makes you desperate for water, to the point you will walk miles to drink it. We will know the church is hungry when our prayer gatherings are packed to capacity, when we no longer look at our watches on Sunday morning during the sermon, and when we can't help but to spend time in God's presence. The good news is that hunger can and must be *developed*. If you don't have it, you can prompt it. If you want this hunger of which I speak, simply ask God to create in you a hunger and a thirst for His presence.

Day 55: Power Prayer

Father, in the name of Jesus, I thank You for the power of Your unfailing Word. I declare that I possess a supernatural hunger and thirst for Your Word and for Your presence. Your Word says, blessed are those who hunger and thirst after righteousness, for they shall be filled. I declare that I hunger and thirst after righteousness. I declare that I am filled with the fullness of almighty God. I declare that my family, my community, my children, and my loved ones are filled with supernatural hunger. I declare that I am no longer content with "church as usual." I declare that I walk in signs, wonders, and miracles according to Your Word. I desire to pursue You with all of my heart. I declare that I am driven by an insatiable desire to manifest Your kingdom in the earth. I declare that the spiritual hunger is contagious, and that everyone who comes into contact with me develops the same hunger and greater. In Jesus' name, amen!

Day 56: Lessons from Lazarus

And when he thus had spoken, he cried with a loud voice, Lazarus, come forth. And he that was dead came forth, bound hand and foot with graveclothes: and his face was bound about with a napkin. Jesus saith unto them, Loose him, and let him go. (John 11:43–44)

n John 11, we read that Jesus was told that Lazarus, Jesus' dear friend, was sick and near to death. You would think that the Lord would rush to his side, but He actually did the very opposite; He waited several days where He was! Have you ever felt like God didn't show up when you wanted Him? This was exactly how Mary and Martha, the sisters of Lazarus, felt when they didn't see Jesus. Jesus waited until *after* Lazarus died and then He went to attend the funeral. Talk about unconventional! When Jesus finally arrived, Martha said to him, "*I know that he [Lazarus] shall rise again in the resurrection at the last day*" (John 11:24). Jesus responded, "*I am the resurrection, and the life: he that believeth in me, though he were dead, yet shall he live*" (verse 25). Martha's faith was limited to a healing miracle, but she did not recognize that Jesus was capable of so much more.

What do you do when something in your life dies? It could be a dead dream, relationship, or ministry. What do you do? Most people wait by the gravesite and mourn the loss of the thing or person they love. This is absolutely normal, but we need to remember that we are people of today, not people of yesterday. Instead of congregating around *what has been*, we should be eager to step into *what will be*—new life, new opportunities, and new blessings!

Notice especially that Jesus said, *"Loose him and let him go!"* Why did He say this? In those days, the deceased would be wrapped in a burial cloth meant for preservation purposes. They were the clothes that symbolized what was old, decaying, and deceased. Many believers are still wearing their grave clothes. They are still living in their past. If you want to walk in the newness of life, you must first be loosed from the attire of the old. Shake off the mentalities of defeat or despair, remember that we serve a resurrected Jesus, and ask for His garments of *new life*!

163

Day 56: Power Prayer

Father, in the name of Jesus, I thank You for Your supernatural favor and grace. Your Word declares that You are the resurrection and the life; therefore, I declare that I receive and walk in the newness of life. Your Word says that if any person be in Christ, they are a new creation; old things are passed away, and all things have become new. I declare that I walk in the new. I declare that old thought patterns, frames of mind, relationships, and behaviors are dead. I take off the "grave clothes" associated with the old man and I put on the garments of my resurrection. I declare that every incriminating thought, suggestion, or imagination that exalts itself against the knowledge of God is cast down in the name of Jesus. I declare that I think differently and embrace a new spiritual paradigm. I am not the same! I am a new creation, born from the Spirit of the living God. I declare that the old has been done away and the new has come into manifestation, in the name of Jesus Christ. Amen!

Day 57: Purify My Heart

Who shall ascend into the hill of the LORD? or who shall stand in his holy place? He that hath clean hands, and a pure heart; who hath not lifted up his soul unto vanity, nor sworn deceitfully. (Psalm 24:3–4)

There was a song we used to sing in church called "Purify My Heart." Essentially, the song was a prayer asking God to cleanse our heart from anything that prevented us from becoming who or what He wanted us to be. This song still resonates with me today. Why is it so important for us to have a pure heart? Because our heart is the repository of our emotions, our will, and our innermost thoughts. Our heart shows what we're living for! King David once wrote, *"Create in me a clean heart, O God; and renew a right spirit within me"* (Psalm 51:10). As New Testament believers, one of the most important aspects of our lives is the condition of our hearts. Jesus said, *"Blessed are the pure in heart: for they shall see God"* (Matthew 5:8).

One day, while in my prayer closet, I had the most miraculous experience. In short, I saw heaven! Whether this was an out-of-body experience or a vision, I can't say, but it felt very real. I was moving faster than the speed of light, and all of a sudden I came to a screeching halt. As I looked ahead, I saw a holy city. It was so beautiful! As I attempted to draw closer, I heard the Lord say, *"Blessed are the pure in heart for they shall see God."* I realized that my heart had become cold toward the things of God, even though I had been heavily involved in ministry. It was then that I realized what Jesus meant by the phrase, *"Blessed are the pure in heart…."* We have to make a conscious decision to have a pure heart. We must ask the Lord to expose the areas in our heart that are displeasing to Him.

What do you think about? What are you meditating on? Whatever you meditate on you will medicate on, and this will always affect your heart. Ask the Lord to purify your heart and cleanse you of anything that will not allow you to see Him clearly.

Day 57: Power Prayer

Father, in the name of Jesus, I thank You for Your mercy and love toward me. Thank You, Lord, for Your everlasting promises. I declare that my heart is cleansed by the power of Your Word. I ask that You forgive me for entertaining thoughts, conversations, and meditations that have affected my heart in a negative way. I ask You to remove anything in my heart or mind that is causing spiritual blockage in my life. I desire to see You; therefore, I ask You to purge me from anything that is not like You. I declare that anything in my heart that was not planted by the Lord Jesus is uprooted by the power of the Holy Spirit. Father, I declare that You are enthroned upon my heart, and there are no other gods before You. I declare that my heart is fixed on the Word of God and the presence of God, in the name of Jesus. Amen!

Day 58: Activate the Grace!

*And God is able to make **all grace** abound toward you;*
that ye, always having all sufficiency in all things, may
abound to every good work. (2 Corinthians 9:8)

One of the most misunderstood subjects in the church is the subject of grace. It has been a topic of much discussion, debate, and at times contention. What is the grace of God? (I discuss this topic in detail in my book *Supernatural Favor.*) There are several connotations of grace in both the Old and New Testament, but essentially grace has two dimensions: unmerited favor and supernatural power. Most people understand grace in the context of God's unmerited favor and goodness toward humanity. This grace was personified in Christ. (See John 1.) However, there is another aspect of grace that people fail to explore, and that is God's supernatural ability working in and through the life of a believer.

In 2 Corinthians, the apostle Paul exclaims, *"And God is able to make all grace abound toward you; that ye, always having all sufficiency in all things, may abound to every good work."* I love the term *"all grace."* It denotes every favor, power, and earthly blessing. The idea is that we have already received the grace of God, but it must be activated in our lives. How do we activate the grace of God? In the book of Ephesians, we read, *"For by grace are ye saved through faith; and that not of yourselves: it is the gift of God"* (Ephesians 2:8). In other words, faith activates the grace for salvation. This must also be true of every manifestation of God's grace in our lives (that is, the grace to be healed, to prosper, and to overcome adversity). Every time we release our faith in God's Word, we activate His grace to meet whatever need we have. When I began to place my faith in His Word, I began to see change and transformation in my life. Why? His grace is sufficient; I simply needed to use it! God wants to manifest His grace in your life as well, but you need to place a demand by faith. The greater the demand, the greater the supply!

Day 58: Power Prayer

Father, in the name of Jesus, I praise You for who You are and all that You have done in my life. I declare that Your unlimited favor and grace abound toward me, that I have all sufficiency in every area of my life. I declare that I lack nothing! I declare that Your supernatural power is working in and through my life right now. My life is a conduit of supernatural favor and divine power. I declare that the grace of almighty God surrounds me like a shield. I declare that I walk in supernatural wisdom, understanding, and ability. I declare that things are easy for me because of the grace of God upon my life. Your grace extends to my family, friends, and community. Just as Jesus grew in favor, wisdom, and stature, I declare that I grow in favor, wisdom, and stature. I will never subject myself to the dictates of this world's system. I am not limited by my income, education, or family background; I walk in unlimited power. My life will never be the same because of Your mighty power in the name of Jesus. Amen!

169

Day 59: Prayers of Vindication

Say to them that are of a fearful heart, Be strong, fear not: behold, your God will come with vengeance, even God with a recompence; he will come and save you. (Isaiah 35:4)

If there is one thing that I have discovered, it is that God is a God of justice. I wish that I could say my ministry journey has been without pain, but I cannot. While in pastoral ministry, I have been through some of the most painful betrayals that I have ever experienced. What do you do when someone you love is literally trying to destroy your character and reputation? At other times, I was downright defrauded financially and otherwise. I can remember one particular occasion when someone whom I trusted betrayed me on a deeply personal level. I was hurt and angry all at the same time. Prior to this, I was accustomed to fixing everything that was broken, but this time I just couldn't fix it! I prayed, and the Lord spoke to me and said, "Stand still and see My salvation. I will vindicate you!"

Unfortunately for us, God has a different idea of vindication than we do. We often want people to pay for the wrong that they have done, but there is a difference between punishment and justice. God is a righteous Judge, who rules with grace and longsuffering. Ultimately, the root of everything He does is redemption. As I waited and prayed, God began to show me things that I didn't know before about the situation, including things that I did wrong. Still, there is a place for imprecation.

We are never to imprecate people, but we are to imprecate the spiritual forces controlling them. I began to pray for the people involved. As I began to pray for them, God began to vindicate them. A few days later, a family member offered to pay our mortgage for the next six months. Hallelujah! The greatest form of vindication is God's favor and blessing upon your life. (I almost felt like telling the Lord that if this is what persecution can bring, keep it coming, but I wouldn't dare pray that prayer!) What about our family members? What about injustice in the world today? God wants us to pray His righteous recompense in the affairs of this life.

Day 59: Power Prayer

Father, in the name of Jesus, I know that You are a God of justice. I stand before the courts of heaven, pleading my cause in the name of Jesus. I declare Your righteous vindication and recompense in every situation in my life. I declare imprecation upon forces of darkness and all workers of iniquity who have been assigned to destroy the righteous. I declare that every trap and snare of the evil one is uncovered and exposed in the name of Jesus. I declare that those who dig a ditch for the innocent will fall into it themselves.

For Finances: I declare that all financial fraud, theft, or deception cease and desist in the name of Jesus. I declare that all illegal debt or usury be released and repaid in the name of Jesus. I declare all contracts satisfied, property returned, and bankruptcy released in the name of Jesus. I declare full financial repayment and restoration in the name of Jesus.

For Marriage: I declare that all marriage-breaking spirits be cast out, and all agents of darkness working against my marriage be exposed and brought to righteous justice, in the name of Jesus. I declare that all properties lost as a result of a court proceeding, lien, or judgment return now. I declare that all losses stop and all embarrassment cease now.

For Family: I declare that every curse spoken against my family (immediate and extended) returns to its sender. I declare that all spiritual attacks are neutralized and all demonic points of contact are exposed now. In the name of Jesus, amen!

Day 60: Confusing the Enemy's Counsel

And Absalom and all the men of Israel said, The counsel of Hushai the Archite is better than the counsel of Ahithophel. For the LORD had appointed to defeat the good counsel of Ahithophel, to the intent that the LORD might bring evil upon Absalom. (2 Samuel 17:14)

Behind every great man is a great counselor. In every place of leadership, whether it is a palace, parliament, or Senate, there is always some form of royal advisement or executive cabinet. Such was the case with King David. His most trusted and wisest advisor was a man named Ahithophel. He was so wise that receiving counsel from him was considered the same as speaking to an oracle of God. (See 2 Samuel 16:23.) Unfortunately, when Absalom revolted against his father David, he took his father's best counselors—including Ahithophel. This was a serious problem! Why? Ahithophel was always right! As long as he was an advisor to Absalom, David would be at a strategic disadvantage. However, there was a solution at hand. It was decided that Hushai the Archite would infiltrate the counselors of Absalom and frustrate the counsel of Ahithophel. (See 2 Samuel 17:14.) The plan worked! God brought judgment on Absalom and Ahithophel, and David's kingdom was restored.

God is about to frustrate the counsel of Ahithophel in your life. Ironically, the name Ahithophel means "my brother is a fool" or "folly." God will turn the counsel against you into folly. You must understand that behind every work of iniquity is an evil counsel. All those who are conspiring against you will be brought to confusion. The Bible declares, *"For the wisdom of this world is foolishness with God. For it is written, He taketh the wise in their own craftiness"* (1 Corinthians 3:19). We are at a strategic advantage because our advisor is the Creator of the universe. Hallelujah! Whoever gathers against you will fall!

Day 60: Power Prayer

Father, in the name of Jesus, I thank You that You are the Creator of the universe. There is no situation or circumstance that happens without Your knowledge. I thank You for Your infinite wisdom, which You have manifested in my life. I declare that the counsel of the evil one is brought to confusion. I declare that every evil device, plot, scheme, or conspiracy is nullified and neutralized. I declare that the counsel of Ahithophel has failed. You take the wise in their own craftiness, therefore, the wisdom of men is mere foolishness before Your mighty counsel. No plan of the enemy will prevail against me or my family, in the name of Jesus. I release every demonic agent from his or her foul assignment in the name of Jesus. I declare that I possess supernatural wisdom. I declare that I am untouchable as far as my enemies are concerned. I dwell under the shadow of His wings, and I am hidden in the secret place of the Most High in the name of Jesus. Amen!

Day 61: Beauty for Ashes

To appoint unto them that mourn in Zion, to give unto them beauty for ashes, the oil of joy for mourning, the garment of praise for the spirit of heaviness; that they might be called trees of righteousness, the planting of the LORD, that he might be glorified. (Isaiah 61:3)

On my first trip to Nigeria, the food, the culture, and the people fascinated me. One part of Nigerian life that I was introduced to was the concept of money changing. In many African countries (and other countries around the world) currency is exchanged on the street by people called moneychangers. Their job is to take your foreign currency and exchange it for the local currency. Well, God is the divine "moneychanger" of the universe; He gives us *"beauty for ashes, the oil of joy for mourning,* [and] *the garment of praise for the spirit of heaviness"* (Isaiah 61:3). He will exchange our ashes for His beauty, our mourning for the oil of joy, and our heaviness for the garment of praise in what I call the "great exchange." These things signify the currency of heaven, and the things we give up are the currency of earth. God is the only currency exchanger that will give you something superior for that which is inferior. What a magnificent God we serve!

Ashes represent the death of something. God is essentially saying, "If you will give me your dead stuff, I will give you something beautiful in exchange." He will take our pain and use it as a means for releasing the anointing of the Holy Spirit. He will exchange our heaviness and despair for a garment of praise. But in order for any exchange to take place, there must first be a release. Too many believers are holding on to their ashes, which is why they have yet to experience the beauty they desire. They are embracing heaviness rather than releasing it to God. Let it go! The moment you let go and open your heart is the moment the great exchange can begin.

Day 61: Power Prayer

Father, in the name of Jesus, I thank You for Your goodness and grace toward me. I thank You for who You are and everything that You have done in my life. I declare that I have received beauty in exchange for ashes. I declare that I am a tree of righteousness. I declare that I am planted in Your kingdom for the glory of God. I declare that I am blessed and prospered according to Your will. I choose to rejoice in Your goodness. I declare that despair, depression, and rejection no longer operate in my life. I remove the garments of sadness and grief, and I put on the garment of praise. I declare that this is my season of rejoicing. I declare that there is a divine shift in my family. I declare that things are turning around in my favor. I declare that praise is my weapon, and I utilize the arsenal to pull down every stronghold of the enemy in the name of Jesus. Amen!

176

Day 62: The Aaronic Blessing

The LORD bless thee, and keep thee: the LORD make his face shine upon thee, and be gracious unto thee: the LORD lift up his countenance upon thee, and give thee peace. (Numbers 6:24–26)

In the book of Numbers chapter 6, God gave Moses a specific prayer for Aaron and his sons. This prayer was to be prayed over the children of Israel. God said that every time this prayer was prayed, His name would be placed upon the Israelites. This prayer is often referred to as the Aaronic blessing. The first time I learned about this prayer was several years ago, through one of my Messianic Jewish friends. Now, every night, I pray this prayer over my children, and every time my congregation gathers together, I pray this over them.

The first part of the blessing is *"the Lord **bless** thee and keep thee."* This is the Hebrew word *barak*, which means "to cause to kneel." This was the same blessing given to Abraham: *"And I will make of thee a great nation, and I will **bless** thee, and make thy name great; and thou shalt be a blessing"* (Genesis 12:2). Kings literally knelt before Abraham. What does it mean to keep us? This is the Hebrew word *shamar*, which means to "guard, keep watch and ward, protect." In other words, this portion of the Aaronic blessing deals with divine protection.

The second portion of the Aaronic blessing is *"the LORD make his face to shine upon thee, and be gracious unto thee."* The picture of God making His face to shine upon us represents the light of His Word. In other words, it represents revelation. His grace is His unmerited favor.

Third, the blessing states, "*The LORD lift up his countenance upon thee, and give thee peace.*" Actually, the word "*countenance*" is also translated "face." It represents counsel or wisdom, as in, seeking the face of someone wise. Lastly, the peace is translated *shalom*, which means "completeness…soundness…prosperity." When you pray this Aaronic blessing with revelation, knowing what each phrase conveys, your life will never be the same.

Day 62: Power Prayer

Father, I thank You for Your grace and goodness toward me. I thank You for who You are and all that You have done. I declare the Aaronic blessing over myself and my loved ones in the name of Jesus. *"The LORD bless thee, and keep thee: the LORD make his face shine upon thee, and be gracious unto thee: the LORD lift up his countenance upon thee, and give thee peace."* I declare that the blessing of Abraham is upon my life. The blessing of the Lord pursues me and overtakes me in the name of Jesus. I declare that I walk under divine protection. I declare that I am illuminated by the revelation of the Father. I declare that the unmerited favor of the Most High surrounds me like a shield, and that I have favor with God and men. I declare that God's divine countenance is lifted upon me, and as a result I walk in divine wisdom and understanding. I declare that the peace and wholeness of God saturates every area of my life in the name of Jesus. Amen!

179

Day 63: Divine Downloads

*Now when much time was spent, and when sailing was now dangerous, because the fast was now already past, Paul admonished them, and said unto them, **Sirs, I perceive that this voyage will be with hurt and much damage**, not only of the lading and ship, but also of our lives.*

(Acts 27:9–10)

In undergraduate school, I studied computer science. It wasn't really my forte, but I thought it would be a great way to make money. (I have since learned that money is one of the worse motives for making any decision, but I digress.) During my undergraduate years, there was an emergence of something called over-the-air downloading. A technology was developed and marketed that allowed you to download software directly to a wireless device. Now most people cannot imagine a world where this was not possible, but back then it was a new and exciting concept.

I want you to imagine for a second that *you* are a mobile device. Now imagine that heaven wants to download information directly to you. In order to receive the download, you need a cellular or other wireless signal. Prayer is the divine connection to heaven that allows us to receive divine downloads from God. Prayer is the signal! Do you have it? Many believers are on "zero" when it comes to their signal strength. Paul, on the other hand, was a man of consistent prayer; as a result, he could receive divine warnings from heaven via direct download. God warned Paul of an impending shipwreck by way of divine download. God is no respecter of persons; He desires to do the same for you and me. All we have to do is get our signal strength up. The beauty is that it doesn't matter how good the reception is in the natural world, we can always establish a connection; simply open your mouth and pray to the Father in the name of Jesus.

Day 63: Power Prayer

Father, I praise You for Your power and might. You are far stronger than the mighty wind; You are far wider than the ocean; You are far greater than the Rockies. Lord, I am like an ant before Your face, and yet You love me! You have called me according to the divine purpose of Your will! Lord, You are more than I can even imagine, and yet You want to enter into a divine partnership with me, because of Your grace. You want to download Your will into my heart. Lord, I am willing! Lord, here I am, send me! I declare that I hear Your voice; I declare that I receive Your signal. I declare that I know things because You have revealed them to me. For Your glory, Lord! And in the name of Your Son, Jesus Christ, amen.

181

Day 64: The Spirit of Reconciliation

> *And all things are of God, who hath reconciled us to himself by Jesus Christ, and hath given to us the ministry of reconciliation; to wit, that God was in Christ, reconciling the world unto himself, not imputing their trespasses unto them; and hath committed unto us the word of reconciliation.* (2 Corinthians 5:18–19)

Everything about the redemptive plan of God centers on His desire to reconcile mankind to Himself. This is expressed so beautifully in this famous verse: *"For God so loved the world, that he gave his only begotten Son, that whosoever believeth in him should not perish, but have everlasting life"* (John 3:16). It was His love for mankind that motivated Him to send His Son, Jesus Christ. This love was solely based on His omni-benevolence and not based on any inherent goodness on our part. Consequently, at the core of all Christian expression is the need and hope for reconciliation. Even prayer itself is based on the spirit of reconciliation. The Bible says, *"God was in Christ, reconciling the world unto himself, not imputing their trespasses unto them; and hath committed unto us the word of reconciliation"* (2 Corinthians 5:19).

We have been called to be ministers of reconciliation. Every time we pray we are executing our ministry of reconciliation. The word *"reconciliation"* means *"to exchange values or to restore to favor."* Through the cross, God restored us to a place of favor with Himself. In turn, we have been called to restore all those around us to a place of favor with God, and one of the ways we accomplish this task is through prayer.

Unfortunately, most believers underestimate the power of prayer. Never doubt that it can turn a situation around! Instead of complaining about that wayward relative or disobedient child, commit them to the Lord in prayer. Declare God's Word over their lives. Call them into alignment with heaven's agenda. Reconcile them! Is there someone who has hurt, wounded, or abandoned you? Pray that they be restored to fellowship with God first, and that your relationship be restored. When Adam dropped the ball in the garden of Eden, God didn't just write him off as a lost cause; He initiated a brilliant plan of redemption. In fact, God knew Adam was going to fall before He even created him (don't ask me how that works). It is time for you and me to step into our ministry of reconciliation.

183

Day 64: Power Prayer

Father, in the name of Jesus Christ of Nazareth, I thank You for who You are and all that You have done in my life. I declare that I am a minister of reconciliation. I recognize that it is Your good pleasure to reconcile the world to Yourself, which is why You sent Your Son, Jesus Christ, to die on the cross. I declare that I am fully and actively engaged in the ministry of reconciliation. I am not just a hearer of Your Word, but I am also a doer of Your Word. I declare that every broken area and dysfunctional situation in my life is restored to order in the name of Jesus. I declare that I walk in love and compassion. I am fully equipped and empowered to minister to others. I am an ambassador of Jesus Christ, and everywhere I go is an embassy of God. Thank you, Lord, for entrusting me with such an awesome ministry. Amen!

Day 65: The Spirit of Prophecy

*And I fell at his feet to worship him. And he said unto me, See thou do it not: I am thy fellowservant, and of thy brethren that have the testimony of Jesus: worship God: for **the testimony of Jesus is the spirit of prophecy**.*

(Revelation 19:10)

Pastor, I am not a prophet!" If I had a quarter for every time I heard this statement, I would be a very rich man! There seems to be two extremes in the body of Christ: those who want titles and those who are running away from them. The truth is that every believer has a prophetic nature whether you go by the title of "prophet" or not. There is such a thing as the office of the prophet, which I will not discuss here. I, however, am not referring to the *office* of the prophet; I am referring to the *spirit* of prophecy.

What is the spirit of prophecy? The Bible says that the spirit of prophecy is the testimony of Jesus Christ. To prophesy is to give a discourse from divine inspiration and to declare the purposes of God. Under this definition, all of us have been called to prophesy. We have been called to share the testimony of Jesus Christ with all those around us. God doesn't just want you to keep your testimony to yourself. What has the Lord done for you? What has He delivered you from? How has He transformed your life? All of these are potentially divinely inspired messages that have the power to impact someone's life to the glory of God!

Earlier, I mentioned the relationship between prayer and our prophetic DNA. One of the most prophetic acts in the New Testament is prayer. Through prayer, men and women of God have received supernatural revelation. Prayer has delivered people from death, demonic conspiracies, and stopped the mouths of lions. This is what I call prophetic prayer. This is the ability to gaze into the unseen realm and make intercession according to the leading of the Holy Spirit. You can make prophetic declarations over your loved ones. The more you become conscious of the prophetic, the more you will begin to release the spirit of prophecy.

Day 65: Power Prayer

Father, in the name of Jesus Christ, I thank You for the power of Your love. I thank You for everything that You have done in my life. I declare that I possess the spirit of prophecy. Today, I unlock my prophetic DNA and I activate the spirit of prophecy within me. The Bible declares that they overcame the devil by the blood of the Lamb, and by the word of their testimony. (See Revelation 12:11.) Therefore, I declare that I possess the testimony of Jesus. I speak to every mountain of adversity and I command it to be removed in the name of Jesus. The Word of God says that we shall decree a thing, and it shall be established. I decree that the Word of God is the final authority in my life. I decree that my prophetic DNA is fully functional and active. I declare that I have acute discernment and I am receptive to the voice of the Holy Spirit in the name of Jesus! Amen!

187

Day 66: Atmospheric Shift

Now when Solomon had made an end of praying, the fire came down from heaven, and consumed the burnt offering and the sacrifices; and the glory of the LORD filled the house. (2 Chronicles 7:1)

I have discovered that prayer has the power to shift atmospheres. An atmosphere is the pervading tone or mood of a place or situation. In fact, every time we pray, we actually invite the atmosphere of heaven *into* the earth. Jesus said, *"After this manner therefore pray ye: Our Father which art in heaven, hallowed be thy name. Thy kingdom come, thy will be done in earth, as it is in heaven"* (Matthew 6:9–10). On one occasion, I was traveling through an airport and I was waiting for a standby seating assignment. There were no seats available on the plane at the time, but it was absolutely critical that I made my flight! The gate agent seemed a bit apathetic toward my situation. By all appearances, there was no way I was going to make it onto that plane. But I learned a long time ago that prayer changes things, and so I directed my thoughts toward God, not toward frustration and worry, and said, "Lord, thank You for Your favor and grace. I thank You for the manifestation of Your presence in this atmosphere."

Shortly afterward, the gate agent looked at me as if she was a different person, and brightly said, "You have a seat assignment." Hallelujah! This is what I call an atmospheric shift.

Prayer has the power to shift the tone, mood, and physical presence of any situation, circumstance, or environment. You can shift the atmosphere of your home, church, school, or place of employment through prayer. Too many believers settle for the way things are in the natural world, not realizing that heaven is waiting on our invitation to come in and renovate the ambience of our life.

When Solomon had finished praying, fire came down from heaven and consumed his offering and sacrifices. If this were possible under the Old Testament, how much more do we, as born-again believers, have the grace and ability to release an atmospheric shift? It is time to bring heaven down to earth!

Day 66: Power Prayer

Father, in the name of Jesus, I thank You for Your power and presence. I declare that Your presence is made manifest in my life. Your Word says that we are to invite the kingdom of heaven upon the earth through prayer. Right now, I declare that Your Spirit, power, and peace are made manifest in the atmosphere of my life. I declare that prayer changes things and situations. I declare that my home, family, church, school, and community experiences a supernatural mega-shift. I declare that the angels of God are released (according to Your Word) to go and minister on my behalf. I declare that the favor and goodness of God literally permeates the atmosphere as we speak, and things are turning around for my good right now! I release Your supernatural presence into every area of my life, in the name of Jesus. I declare that all strife, confusion, and chaos must disperse right now. I command order and purpose to manifest *now*. I declare that the atmosphere of heaven fills my life in the name of Jesus. Amen!

Day 67: Your Whole House
Shall Be Saved

And they said, Believe on the Lord Jesus Christ, and thou
shalt be saved, and thy house. (Acts 16:31)

God is very concerned with families. He was so concerned
with the condition of families, that He sent Jesus Christ
to restore His family. At the heart of God's eternal purpose is
the reconciliation and restoration of relationships. He gave His
life to restore a broken relationship with His own children. If
God would go to such lengths to restore fallen humanity, what
makes you think that He is not ardently concerned about your
family? I want to submit to you that God loves your family more
than you do!

The Bible says, *"And Jesus said unto him, This day is salvation
come to this house, forsomuch as he also is a son of Abraham"* (Luke
19:9). As children of Abraham (through Jesus), we have received
the promise of salvation for our entire family. Just like all promises, you will never enjoy them if you refuse to believe them.
The Bible says in Acts, *"And they said, Believe on the Lord Jesus
Christ, and thou shalt be saved, and thy house"* (Acts 16:31). The
moment you placed your faith and trust in Christ, your family became a recipient of the promise of salvation. I don't know
about you but I refuse to go to heaven without my entire family.
There is nothing Satan can do about it! I am so adamant about
their salvation that I will resurrect a dead loved one just to make

sure they prayed the prayer of salvation. Do not allow the devil to discourage you in this area. Maybe your family (immediate or extended) may not be serving God right now, but they will; Jesus promises you that they will! Be encouraged!

Day 67: Power Prayer

Father, I thank You for Your eternal goodness. There is no one like You in the entire universe. You are the Creator and Ruler of the world. I declare that the promise of salvation has come to my entire house. I declare that my entire family is born again, Spirit-filled, and on their way to heaven. I break the power off of the mind of my loved ones who have yet to make Jesus their Lord. I declare that all spiritual blindness has been lifted, and the power of God is made manifest to them. I declare that my whole house shall be saved in the name of Jesus. I mark every member in my family with the blood of Jesus, and I declare that they are the legal property of heaven. I declare that the power and presence of God surrounds my bloodline. I have a good heritage in the earth. I declare that from this day forward, my family is a Jesus family. I declare that every person in my family loves Jesus with all of their heart. Thank You, Lord, for saving my entire house in the name of Jesus. Amen!

Day 68: Live and Not Die!

I shall not die, but live, and declare the works of the
LORD. (Psalm 118:17)

Several years ago, my wife and I were ministering at an Assemblies of God church in Florida. We were standing near the altar and praying for the sick. There were several people in the audience who were suffering from chronic ailments. There was one particular lady who came forward. She told us that both she and her husband had retired from ministry as a result of sickness. Her husband had been diagnosed with cancer, and underwent surgery to remove cancerous tissue from his throat. Now she was very concerned because cancerous growths were appearing all over her body, and she suspected it was melanoma. As she came forward, I was about to lay hands on her and pray, but the Lord said, "No!" He said, "Tell her that she will live and not die!" In obedience, I spoke those very words, and as I did, the power and presence of God came over her. It was as if someone threw a ton of bricks on top of us! Being overwhelmed, she fell under the power of God, and began to weep uncontrollably. Afterward, she came to me and thanked me for praying with her.

I thought that this was a very wonderful experience, but it didn't stop there. A couple of days later, she contacted my wife to tell us that the cancerous growths on her body had withered and fallen off her body. Hallelujah! This is what you call a miracle! The words that I spoke over this precious woman were in fact a prophetic decree that was filled with supernatural power. David spoke these very words over himself in his darkest hour. (See Psalm 118:17.) There are times when it is appropriate to pray, but there are times when we need to prophesy. What area in your life seems plagued with the threat of death? Is it your health? Is it your marriage? Declare, "I will live and not die and declare the works of the Lord!" Prophesy to yourself and to the people you love. Tell that relative or friend, "You will not die, but live…"

Day 68: Power Prayer

194

Father, in the name of Jesus, I praise You for who You are and all that You have done. I declare that I will not die, but live, and declare the works of the Lord. I declare that the power of God will be made manifest in my life. I declare that it is well with me! I declare that I have passed from death to life, because Jesus is my Lord. I declare that sickness, disease, and destruction must leave me now. I declare that the spirit of death is broken off of my loved ones, as well as myself. The law of the Spirit of life in Christ Jesus has freed me from the law of sin and death, therefore sickness and death have no place in me or in the lives of those I love. Your Word declares that with long life You will satisfy me and show me Your salvation. (See Psalm 91:16.) I declare that it is well with my soul, in the name of Jesus. I will never fear death again, because I possess eternal life in the name of Jesus. Amen!

Day 69: Make Room for Your Miracle

And it fell on a day, that Elisha passed to Shunem, where was a great woman; and she constrained him to eat bread. And so it was, that as oft as he passed by, he turned in thither to eat bread. And she said unto her husband, Behold now, I perceive that this is an holy man of God, which passeth by us continually. Let us make a little chamber, I pray thee, on the wall; and let us set for him there a bed, and a table, and a stool, and a candlestick: and it shall be, when he cometh to us, that he shall turn in thither.

(2 Kings 4:8–10)

One of my favorite Bible stories is this account of Elisha and the Shunamite woman. This woman noticed that the man of God passed by her every day, so she convinced him to eat bread at her residence. The woman eventually even convinced her husband to build a small apartment for Elisha. As a result of her kindness, Elisha called the woman (through his servant Gehazi) and asked her what she wanted. She replied, in short, that she could not conceive a child; Elisha prophesied to her that she would have a child by the very next year. Glory to God!

There are many powerful dynamics to this story, but the one I want to draw the most attention to is that the Shunamite woman made room for her miracle. How did she make room for her miracle? The woman discerned that Elisha was a man of God, and that he carried the presence and power of God. By making room for him she was in fact making room for the miraculous power of God in her life. She inconvenienced herself for the sake of God's holy man, and God rewarded her.

What miracle are you expecting from God? What is it that you want God to do in your life? The apartment represents our hearts. Have you made room in your heart? Too many people are asking God for a miracle, but they haven't made room for Him to work in their lives. Put God to the test! Open the doors of your heart and let Him in. I often tell people that the attitude of expectancy is the atmosphere for the miraculous. Are you anticipating a miracle? Every day that I wake up, I expect God to do something supernatural in my life. I demonstrate this expectation by accommodating the very thing that I want God to do. One time, I believed God for a new car. I began to prepare for a brand new car; I researched insurance quotes and car accessories even though in the natural, I didn't have the money to afford a car. To my surprise, someone decided to give my wife and I cash to buy a car. Praise the Lord! What do you need God to do for you? Have you made room for it yet?

Day 69: Power Prayer

Father, in the name of Jesus, I thank You for who You are and all that You have done. I declare that You are good and Your mercy endures forever. I declare that Your miraculous power shall be revealed in my life. I declare that my heart is enlarged, and I am confidently expecting You to move in my life with great anticipation. I declare that I walk in Your miraculous power in every area of my life. I declare that You have room in my life and in my heart to manifest Your power and grace. I declare that Your plan for my life is awesome. I am excited about the promises and blessings that You have in store for me. I open my spiritual eyes to divine opportunities. I open my spiritual ears to hear what the Holy Spirit is saying to me at all times. I declare that Your goodness and grace is my guide. I receive my miracle now, in the name of Jesus. Amen!

Day 70: All Things Are Possible

But Jesus beheld them, and said unto them, With men this is impossible; but with God all things are possible.

(Matthew 19:26)

If you haven't realized it by now, we serve a miraculous God who is capable of doing the impossible in our lives. I have seen countless miracles throughout my life and ministry. In fact, no one can ever convince me that God is not real. I have seen too much! This is what sets Christianity apart from any other spiritual expression. Everything about our faith in God centers on the resurrection. God accomplished the most impossible feat two thousand years ago, when He raised our Lord from the dead. If God could raise Jesus from the dead through the power of the Holy Spirit, then there is nothing that He cannot do in our lives. This should make you very excited! Why? Because it doesn't matter where you are in your life; things can change!

Jesus told the man whose son was oppressed by a demonic spirit that *"If thou canst believe, all things are possible to him that believeth"* (Mark 9:23). In the natural world, this man saw no solution, but Jesus is Master of the impossible. If we will simply release our faith in the power of God, we, too, will see miracles in our lives. Most people limit God to what they can figure out through reason and logic. Beloved, God is not a God of reason and logic (though there is a place for these things); He is the God of the supernatural. The supernatural trumps reason and logic every time! Notice that Jesus did not say, *"some* things were possible."* No, He said, *"All things are possible."* The word *"possible"* here is the Greek word *dunatos,* which means "powerful, mighty, [and] strong." In other words, the power of God is sufficient enough to deal with any situation, trial, problem, or circumstance. The more we become conscious of His power, the more impossibilities will become possibilities. This is a decision that every believer must make, a decision based on faith in the Word of God. I challenge you today to believe God! Take Him at His Word, and watch things turn around in your life. I have seen so many situations turn around in my life, and I know that God is no respecter of persons. If He did it for me, He will do it for you!

Day 70: Power Prayer

Father, in the name of Jesus Christ, I know that You are the God of impossibilities. There is nothing that is impossible with You, and all things are possible to those who believe. I choose to believe Your Word. I make a faith decision to be unmoved by what I see or feel; I choose to only be moved by the Word of God. I declare that every impossible situation in my life is turning around for my good and for Your glory. My life will never be the same again because of the manifestation of Your supernatural power. I will never be a slave to reason and logic again. I will not limit You to my finite vantage point, but I recognize that You see all things. I declare that I am no longer trapped in the prison of impossibility, but I am free to believe Your Word. I declare that the impossible has become possible in my life in the name of Jesus. Amen!

200

Day 71: The Glory of God

That they all may be one; as thou, Father, art in me, and I in thee, that they also may be one in us: that the world may believe that thou hast sent me. And the glory which thou gavest me I have given them; that they may be one, even as we are one.   (John 17:21–22)

There is nothing more powerful and profound than the glory of God. We see allusions to God's glory all throughout the Bible, in both the Old and New Testaments. What is the glory of God? The word *"glory"* is derived from a Hebrew word which means "dignity, honor, [and] reputation." Every time the presence of God is made manifest, God is displaying His character and reputation. The rabbinical scholars would refer to this phenomenon as the Shekinah glory of God, which literally meant the manifestation of God's awesome presence in the earthly realm. In the Old Testament, exposure to the glory of God could actually kill in certain instances. However, in the New Testament, God has chosen to manifest His glory *within* us, via the Holy Spirit.

Have you ever thought about the implications of carrying the glory of God on the inside? You are what I call a "glory carrier!" In the New Testament, the word *"glory"* comes from the Greek *doxa*, which means "splendor...brightness...[or] majesty." The same idea is conveyed by Paul the apostle, *"What? know ye not that your body is the temple of the Holy Ghost which is in you, which ye have of God, and ye are not your own?"* (1 Corinthians 6:19). The word *"temple"* here means "sacred edifice." It is akin to the Holy of Holies in the Old Testament tabernacle. In other words, our bodies are the tabernacle of dwelling place for the splendor, majesty, character, and reputation of God. Now that is a conversation starter! "Hey, did you know that the Creator of the universe lives inside me?" Most believers are not conscious of the glory of God, and this is why they don't often recognize or appreciate it. One night I was praying, and the glory of God literally invaded my room. I was speechless! There were no words to articulate how awesome this experience was. This is the same presence that dwells in us. It is time for you to release the glory within you!

202

Day 71: Power Prayer

Father, in the name of Jesus Christ, I thank You for being the God of glory. You are the God of all creation. I declare that Your glory and manifest presence fills my entire being right now. I declare that I am a carrier of Your presence. I declare that everyone in my family is a glory carrier. I recognize that Your reputation is impeccable; therefore, I walk worthy of the glory which You have manifested within me. I declare that my body is the temple of the Holy Spirit. I am Your sacred edifice, and I yield to You completely. Have Your way in me, Lord! I declare that I am a vessel of honor, and that I am fit for the Master's use. I declare that everyone who comes into contact with me, comes into contact with the true and living God, in the name of Jesus. Amen!

Day 72: Just Believe!

Therefore I say unto you, What things soever ye desire,
when ye pray, believe that ye receive them, and ye shall have
them. (Mark 11:24)

Just believe! This seems like a very over-simplified statement, doesn't it? But the truth is this statement is one of the most powerful statements you have ever heard. Why? The key to experiencing the supernatural power of God is *believing*. The Bible says that if we believe when we pray, we will receive that which we ask for. The church has done a great job of complicating this issue. We often put stipulations on prayer that Jesus never gave us. What Jesus said is really quite simple: *"Therefore I say to you, whatever things you ask when you pray, believe that you receive them, and you will have them"* (NKJV). The question is: what do you desire from God today? Do you believe? If you will dare to believe, then you will definitely receive!

What does it mean to believe? To believe something simply means to accept it as true. Think about the things that you accept as the truth. For example, when you wake up in the morning and swing your feet out of bed, you never question whether the ground is going to fall out from underneath your feet. Why? Because you believe that the ground is a sure foundation. You accept this as the truth. What would happen if we approached the Word of God with the same confidence? Beloved, you must understand that the Word of God is a firm foundation. In fact, the Word of God is a firmer foundation than the physical floor that you're standing on right now. If you will believe the Word of God, you will see the glory of God manifested in your life. It does not matter what the situation may be, the key to seeing your miracle is *believing*. I often say that right believing equates to right receiving. What you believe will determine what you receive! Make the decision today to believe God. I promise you will not regret it!

Day 72: Power Prayer

Father, in the name of Jesus Christ, I thank You that Your Word is true, and I recognize that Your Word is the final authority in my life. I declare that You are a supernatural God. I recognize that there is nothing impossible for You. I am a believer in Your Word. Grace is the revelation of God's Word and action; therefore, I am a doer of Your Word and not just a hearer only. You said in Your Word that whatever I desire when I pray, I should believe that I receive it and I will have it. Therefore, I believe that I receive every promise in Your Word. I declare that I am blessed! I declare that I have more than enough! I declare that I lack nothing in my life. I declare that I am healed! I declare that I am delivered! I declare that I am a believer and not a doubter. By faith, I receive the promise of victory in my life in the name of Jesus. Amen!

Day 73: Don't Look Back

*But his wife looked back from behind him, and she became
a pillar of salt.* (Genesis 19:26)

There is nothing more hazardous to our spiritual growth than
looking back. In fact, everything about the Christian life is
about moving forward and upward in God. He does not want
us to be stagnated by looking at the past. We can see this in the
graphic story of Lot's wife as she fled with Lot and their children
away from flaming Sodom and Gomorrah. As they ran, Lot's
wife, likely full of regret to leave it behind, looked back—and
she became a pillar of salt! Beloved, this is not some children's
fairytale; this actually occurred!

What was the significance of the pillar of salt? The pillar
of salt represents bitterness, and this is exactly what happens
when you and I look back instead of looking forward. We run
the risk of becoming bitter. Beloved, God doesn't want you bitter, because bitterness leads to barrenness. Nothing can grow
or flourish in a salty place. Think of the Dead Sea in Israel. It
is called the Dead Sea because there is nothing that can live in
that body of water. Why? Because of the high salt content! God
has not called us to be a Dead Sea, He has called us to be a river
of living water. The moment we look back, our waters become
stale and stagnant. However, the moment we move forward,
the power, presence, and purpose of God begins to flow in our
lives.

I don't know about you, but I refuse to look back. I choose to move forward and upward in God. This is the only way to experience a prosperous Christian life. Remember, whatever you gaze upon, you gravitate toward. This is why the Bible tells us in Hebrews 12:2 that we must look unto Jesus, *the author and finisher of our faith.* Beloved, do not look back. Make the decision today that you will be fruitful, prosperous, and successful in the things of God.

Day 73: Power Prayer

Father, in the name of Jesus, I thank You that You are the God of the entire universe. I recognize that Your plan for me is a good plan. Your Word declares in Jeremiah 29:11 that You know the plans that You have for me, and they are plans of good and not of evil. I declare that I am moving forward in You. I refuse to look back! I refuse to become bitter. I have considered Lot's wife, and I have chosen not to emulate her folly. Everything good for my life is ahead of me, and not behind me. I will look unto You, Jesus, as the Author and the Finisher of my faith. I will gaze upon Your face and move forward in my destiny. I choose to let go of all hurts, disappointments, and regrets in the name of Jesus. I freely forgive all those who have hurt or wounded me, as an act of my free will, and in obedience to the Word of God. Thank You, Lord, for a bright and flourishing future, which You have set before me today. I will never look back. I will never be afraid. I will never rehearse the past! I embrace the purpose and plan that You have ordained for my life, and the lives of my loved ones. Amen!

207

Day 74: Arise and Shine

Arise, shine; for thy light is come, and the glory of the Lord
is risen upon thee.   (Isaiah 60:1)

I believe that this is the time for the church to shine like never
before. The Bible tells us that God wants a glorious bride,
without spot or blemish. In other words, Jesus is not coming
back for a church that is busted and disgusted. He is coming
back for a victorious church that exudes the brightness of the
kingdom of God. I don't know about you, but I prefer the latter.
The Bible tells us in the book of Isaiah, *"Arise and shine for your
light is come, and the glory of the* Lord *is risen upon you."* Jesus
told us to let our light shine before men, that they will see our
good works and glorify our heavenly Father. This is the prophetic season to arise! God is waiting on us to reveal the glory of
God to the nations of the earth.

You may have been in a posture of despair or a position
of despondency. The Spirit of the Lord is saying to you, "arise
and shine!" It is time for the church to wake up from spiritual slumber and apathy. It is time for us to become the glorious
bride that Christ says we already are. This is not the time to bow
down and be defeated; this is the time to rise up and take our
place in the kingdom of God. Your season of defeat is over! Your
season of despair has come to a close! This is your time to shine!
I believe that God wants to use you as a burning ember in His
hand to ignite His will and purpose in the earthly realm. You

are not insignificant; rather, you are mighty light in the kingdom of God that He has ordained to manifest the culture of heaven to everyone around you. The glory of the Lord has risen upon your life. This is the character of God! He has placed His character and reputation upon you so that when people see you, they will see Him.

Day 74: Power Prayer

Father, in the name of Your Son, Jesus Christ, I thank You for who You are and all that You have done. I thank You that You have not left us in darkness. I thank You that You *are* light, the light of the world, that You shine brighter than the sun, and that by Your light, we can see our own need for You and we can see the world's need for You. Lord, You promised in Your Word that if we follow Your Son, we shall not walk in darkness but shall have light (see John 8:12); therefore, I declare that darkness is a thing of my past! I declare that I see by Your light, and You light the way before me. I declare that Your light is shining within me, and that I light my family's paths, my friends' paths, my neighbors' paths. I declare that I do not spread darkness, but that today I will *arise and shine* with the glory of Your presence in me, through the saving power of Your Son! In Jesus' name, amen!

Day 75: Light Up the Darkness

This then is the message which we have heard of him, and declare unto you, that God is light, and in him is no darkness at all.   (1 John 1:5)

As I have previously mentioned, one of the responsibilities of the New Testament believer is to dispel the darkness around them. How do we accomplish this? Simply put, we must let our light shine. John the apostle wrote: *"And the light shineth in darkness; and the darkness comprehended it not"* (John 1:5). The word "comprehend" is the Greek word *katalambanō*. This is a compound word denoting, "to seize upon, take possession of,…[or] overtake." In other words, the darkness could not seize nor overtake the light, because the light is superior to the darkness. That's right! The light in you is superior to the darkness around you. That should make you excited! Light represents truth and moral excellence, whereas darkness represents spiritual blindness, ignorance, and immorality.

From the very beginning of creation, God has always made a clear distinction between light and darkness. In Genesis chapter 1, the Bible says, *"And God said, Let there be light: and there was light. And God saw the light, that it was good: and God divided the light from the darkness"* (Genesis 1:3–4). In the Hebrew, this is expressed as "Light be!" The implication is that the light already *was* in God. He literally released the light into the darkness, and the darkness had to scatter. In the same way, God has called you and me as His children to light up the darkness in our families, communities, and relationships. It is time for you to declare, "Light be, in the name of Jesus!" Too many believers are afraid of darkness rather than exercising authority over it. Remember, you cannot exercise authority over something you fear. In order to take dominion over the spiritual darkness around us, we must first recognize that what lives inside of us is greater than anything on the outside. John later expresses is this way: *"Ye are of God, little children, and have overcome them: because greater is he that is in you, than he that is in the world"* (1 John 4:4). You are the light of the world; now let your light shine!

Day 75: Power Prayer

Father, in the name of Jesus, I thank You that You have signed the glorious light of the gospel of Jesus Christ into my heart. I declare that I no longer dwell in darkness. Your Word is a lamp unto my feet, and a light unto my path. I declare that the light of Your truth floods my soul. I will never walk in darkness again, because Jesus lives on the inside of me. I declare that Your light is superior to any darkness in my life. I will never walk in ignorance or spiritual blindness again. Instead, I walk in the fullness of Your truth in every area of my life. I walk in Your divine power and moral excellence. I command all darkness to flee from me now. I declare that darkness, in any form it may manifest, must leave my life and the lives of those I love. Jesus is the light of the world; therefore, I am the light of the world. I declare that the light of Your love flows in and through me to everyone around me in the name of Jesus. Amen!

Day 76: Gideon's Army

And the LORD said unto Gideon, The people that are with thee are too many for me to give the Midianites into their hands, lest Israel vaunt themselves against me, saying, Mine own hand hath saved me. (Judges 7:2)

I f there is one thing that I love, it is a good underdog story. I think it has to do with the fact that I was very short growing up, and I often got picked on. In fact, I learned to fight at an early age, because bigger kids would often try to intimidate me. As you can imagine, there is a soft place in my heart for the "underdog." One of my favorite underdog stories is the biblical account of Gideon and his army of three hundred. Three hundred doesn't seem like such a small number until you compare it to the 135,000-strong Midianite army they were up against. Initially, Gideon had 32,000 men, but God decided that his army was too many. Already outmatched, Gideon's army was ultimately reduced to three hundred men. (See Judges 7:1–11.)

Why did God reduce the army to such a small number? The Bible says, *"The people that are with thee are too many for me to give the Midianites into their hands, lest Israel vaunt themselves against me, saying, Mine own hand hath saved me"* (Judges 7:2). God did not want Israel to be able to take credit for the victory. He didn't want them to boast in the number of soldiers, but in His supernatural power. The same is true in our lives. God will often wait until you are at the point of seeming insufficiency before He steps in, in order that He alone will be glorified. God is raising up a prophetic army of people whom most would consider underdogs. They will be homemakers, schoolteachers, students, grocery store clerks, and factory workers. But however they appear to others, these people have been hand-picked by God to manifest His power in the earth. Gone are the days of name brands and Christian celebrities; God desires to use everyday people to take the world by storm. God wants you to know that it is not by might, nor by power, but by His Spirit. (See Zechariah 4:6.) You will not be able to take the credit, but God will be able to take the glory!

Day 76: Power Prayer

Father, in the name of Jesus Christ, I thank You for who You are and all that You have done in my life. I thank You that You are the God of all creation. Your Word will never return void, but will always accomplish what You sent it to do. I declare that it is not by might nor by power, but by Your Spirit, Lord God. You are the God of the underdog! Just as Gideon defeated an army of 135,000 soldiers, so You will use me to manifest spiritual victory in the affairs of this life. I will not be dismayed by the apparent odds against me. Your Word declares that faith is the substance of things hoped for and the evidence of things not seen. I declare that I walk in bold faith and confidence in Your Word. As a result of my faith in Your Word, nothing is impossible unto me. I believe that Your miraculous power is always at work in me and through me to the glory of God. I cannot lose, because I am more than a conqueror through Him that loves me. I stand victorious in the midst of every spiritual battle in my life, because I trust in Your Word, and I rely upon Your supernatural power in the name of Jesus. Amen!

215

Day 77: Casting Down Imaginations

> *Casting down imaginations, and every high thing that exalteth itself against the knowledge of God, and bringing into captivity every thought to the obedience of Christ.*
>
> (2 Corinthians 10:5)

In grade school, I was a very serious daydreamer. I could not think of anything more excruciating than sitting in that prison they called a classroom. As a right-brain dominant thinker (the hemisphere responsible for creativity), I never had a problem dreaming up all sorts of images, pictures, and scenes. Sometimes I was starring in a Kung-Fu movie, other times I was escaping in a dramatic car chase—no matter the details, my mind was always creating fantastic dreams.

You may not have struggled with daydreaming like me, but as a believer you can probably identify with the battle that we all face in our minds. I believe that the mind is actually the *primary* battlefield of the Christian life. Even though we are born again, we must appropriate the Word of God in our lives by thinking differently. The Bible calls this "mind renewal." Paul the apostle admonished us, *"(For the weapons of our warfare are not carnal, but mighty through God to the pulling down of strong holds;) casting down imaginations, and every high thing that exalteth itself against the knowledge of God, and bringing into captivity every thought to the obedience of Christ"* (2 Corinthians 10:4–5). The key to living a victorious Christian life is learning how to cast down imaginations.

What does the Bible mean by imagination? The word *"imaginations"* comes from the Greek word *logismos*, which means "reasoning: such as is hostile to the Christian faith." In other words, imaginations are images in our mind that have a reason, logic, or philosophy attached to them. For instance, a person who has been abused might carry an image of abuse in their mind. This image may communicate to them that they are unworthy and unloved. The Bible says that we must "cast down" these images, because they are contrary to the Word of God and therefore pose a threat to our spiritual, mental, and emotional well-being. The phrase *"casting down"* literally means "to demolish." Just like a demolition crew will use dynamite to collapse an old, dilapidated building, so the Word of God is the dynamite that tears down outdated and dilapidated thought patterns. The more we meditate on the Word of God, the more we can demolish the thought structures of the enemy.

Day 77: Power Prayer

Father, I thank You for who You are and all that You have done in my life and the lives of those I love. I declare that I possess the mind of Christ. I declare that every thought that is contrary to the Word of God and that contradicts the person of Jesus Christ is cast down, dismantled, and demolished right now in the name of Jesus. I take every thought captive to the obedience of Christ. I declare that every satanic infrastructure erected in my mind must come down now. I declare that every incriminating thought, reasoning, argument, logic, or accusation that exalts itself against the knowledge of God is broken. I cast down every mental and emotional stronghold in my life. I reject every thought rooted in fear, insecurity, or bitterness in the name of Jesus. I only accept thoughts that align with the Word of God. I declare that I am transformed by the renewing of my mind in the name of Jesus. Amen!

Day 78: Walking in Love

For in Jesus Christ neither circumcision availeth any thing,
nor uncircumcision; but faith which worketh by love.
(Galatians 5:6)

There is an inextricable relationship between faith and love. There is nothing that you or anyone can do to change this. In fact, without love, our faith cannot work. The reason why so many people are not seeing the supernatural power of God demonstrated in their lives is because they are missing the main ingredient. What is that main ingredient? The love of God. You must understand, everything God does in our lives is a result of His unconditional love for us. It doesn't matter whether it is healing, deliverance, or supernatural provision, the motivation is the same: the love of God.

What does it mean to walk in love? Essentially, to walk in love is to walk in the nature, character, and mind-set of God toward other people. The word *"love"* comes from the Greek word *agape*, which means "divine love or unconditional love." This love is not based upon the way people treat or respond to us, but is based solely upon the Word of God. Now I know that there are many different types of love expressed in Scripture, such as brotherly love or the love between a husband and a wife. But for the believer, *agape* love must be at the core of everything that we do and say. If you want to see miracles, turn your love on! If you want to see breakthrough, turn your love on! If you want to walk in the supernatural every day of your life, you must commit to walking in and releasing the love of almighty God. The Bible tells us plainly that spiritual gifts without love are useless. In fact, the Bible says that without love we are nothing. Love is long-suffering, kind, and forbearing; love does not think ill toward other people. (See 1 Corinthians 13.)

I have news for you, if your discernment or prophetic gifting is not rooted in love, it's not rooted in God. Make the decision to walk in love today, and the Holy Spirit will make sure that your decision becomes a reality.

Day 78: Power Prayer

Father, in the name of Jesus, I thank You for who You are and all that You have done in my life. I declare that I walk in the love of God. I am filled with Your love. The Holy Spirit sheds the love of God abroad in my heart. I declare that bitterness and resentment have no place in my heart. I received Your *agape* love right now in the name of Jesus. I declare that the miraculous power of God is manifested in my life because Your love is a reality in my spirit. I recognize that Your love is unconditional; therefore, I freely forgive all those who have wounded or hurt me. Your Word declares that love keeps no record of wrong; therefore, I release all offenses, debts, and transgressions right now in the name of Jesus. I declare that I am full of Your love. Your love overflows in and through me. Your Word declares that faith operates by love; therefore, I declare that my faith is functioning properly because it is being energized by the unconditional love of God. I thank You for demonstrating Your love toward me and teaching me how to love others unconditionally in the name of Jesus. Amen!

221

Day 79: Prayers for Family

And if it seem evil unto you to serve the Lord, choose you this day whom ye will serve; whether the gods which your fathers served that were on the other side of the flood, or the gods of the Amorites, in whose land ye dwell: but as for me and my house, we will serve the Lord. (Joshua 24:15)

I have said it on many occasions and I will say it again: nothing is more important to God than family. In fact, the whole body of Christ is God's heavenly family represented in the earth. God is concerned about our families. He wants to intervene in the affairs of our family members. But the question remains, how do we pray for our family? This is a very important question, because it will determine how much and how often you see the Lord move in the lives of your family members. Contrary to popular belief, God doesn't just do things because it is His will. God desires to partner with His children in the earth to see His will coming to fruition in the lives of His people.

The first key to seeing the Holy Spirit moving your family is committing to praying for your family. Again, how do you pray? In the book of Joshua chapter 24, we see the prophet Joshua making a very bold declaration: *"As for me and my house we will serve the Lord."* This is a very simple yet powerful prayer to pray over your family members. The more you pray for your family, the more you will feel a burden of compassion for your family members.

Another aspect of praying for your family is focusing on your family health and well-being by praying words such as, "I declare that my family is healed according to first Peter 2:25. Jesus bore my family's sicknesses and diseases, and with His stripes, they are healed, in the name of Jesus. Amen!" Ask the Lord to teach you how to pray for your family. With fervent and devout prayer, I believe that your family is about to experience a supernatural turnaround.

Day 79: **Power Prayer**

Father, in the name of Jesus, I thank You for who You are and all that You have done in my life. I thank You, Father, for protecting and watching over my family members. I thank You that Your will concerning my family is good. Your Word declares in Jeremiah 29:11 that the plans that You have for me are plans of good and not of evil; therefore, I declare that Your plan for my family is a good plan. I declare that it is well with my family. I declare that my entire house serves the Lord. I declare that my family is united, they are peaceful, and they are Spirit-filled in the name of Jesus. I declare that any chaos operating in my family or anywhere in my bloodline must cease and desist right now, in the name of Jesus. I declare that my family is a family of love and acceptance. I declare that my family is healed and whole according to 1 Peter 2:24. I declare that the culture of heaven permeates everyone in my family. I declare that the blessing, prosperity, and power of God are made manifest in our lives. I declare that anyone in my family who has not made Jesus Christ their Lord and Savior, makes Him their Lord right now. I declare that I have the family from heaven in the name of Jesus. Amen!

Day 80: Release the Supernatural

But if the Spirit of him that raised up Jesus from the dead dwell in you, he that raised up Christ from the dead shall also quicken your mortal bodies by his Spirit that dwelleth in you. (Romans 8:11)

he church has committed a serious crime. We have been guilty of kidnapping. Who has the churched kidnapped? The church has kidnapped the Holy Spirit! Two thousand years ago, on the day of Pentecost, Jesus sent the Holy Spirit to the earth to anoint, equip, and empower the church to fulfill Mark 16:15, which reads *"Go therefore into all the world and preach the gospel to every creature"* (NKJV). Instead of fulfilling this mandate, however, we have relegated the Holy Spirit to the four corners of the church. It is as if we visit Him on Sundays, and leave Him locked in the church until our next visit.

I am being quite facetious, as we all know that the Holy Spirit is omnipresent, but I am hoping to unveil a pervasive mentality in the body of Christ today. We often pray prayers like, "Holy Spirit, come!" when, in fact, He already came two thousand years ago. Paul wrote, *"What? know ye not that your body is the temple of the Holy Ghost which is in you, which ye have of God, and ye are not your own?"* (1 Corinthians 6:19). The Bible says that our bodies are a *"temple"* not a *"prison."* In other words, the Holy Spirit wants out! He wants to touch every fabric of your life. However, He is a gentleman, and even though

He is omnipotent, He always awaits an invitation. Many people are waiting on God to experience the miraculous, when, in fact, the miraculous is already within them. It is time for the church to stop *asking* for the supernatural and start *releasing* the supernatural.

This revelation literally transformed my life and ministry. I stopped waiting on God to move, and I finally went out and actually did what the Bible said. How can you ever see a healing if you never pray for the sick? It is time for us to release the power of God within us. Today would be a good day to start!

Day 80: Power Prayer

Father, in the name of Jesus Christ, I thank You for who You are and all that You've done in my life. I declare that I have a supernatural heritage. I declare that the Holy Spirit dwells and lives on the inside of me. I am full of the Holy Spirit, and therefore full of supernatural power. My body is the temple of the Holy Spirit who lives and dwells within. I declare that the supernatural power of God is made manifest in me. I release miracles right now. I declare that signs, wonders, and miracles are commonplace in my life. I release healing power over every person that I have come into contact with. I declare that the same Spirit who raised Jesus from the dead dwells in me and makes me alive. I declare that my life will never be stagnant, boring, or mundane, because the very Creator of the universe lives on the inside of me. I declare that the same Spirit who, in the beginning of Creation, was the agent of the manifested universe, lives and speaks through me daily. I am excited about the opportunity to minister the supernatural power of God to every person that You have placed in my life, Lord. I declare that miraculous revival begins with me in the name of Jesus. Amen!

Day 81: Spiritual Warfare

For we wrestle not against flesh and blood, but against principalities, against powers, against the rulers of the darkness of this world, against spiritual wickedness in high places.   (Ephesians 6:12)

Many years ago I picked up a book about spiritual warfare and deliverance. I won't name the book, but I will say that after I finished this particular book, I was more afraid of demons than before I started! Unfortunately, this has long been the reputation of the deliverance ministry. Most people view deliverance and spiritual warfare as something scary, and therefore avoid it at all costs. The truth is that spiritual warfare is not scary at all, but is a very important component to the Christian life. If we don't understand spiritual warfare, then it will be difficult for us to walk in constant victory in our lives.

There are some people who are too extreme in their theology concerning spiritual warfare—even rebuking the cream in their coffee because they thought it took a demonic shape! Of course, this is the exception and not the rule. Many people, on the other hand, simply try to ignore the devil. This is a very dangerous mind-set, too. You must understand, beloved, that the devil will not leave you alone just because you ignore him. God wants us to be very balanced in our thinking. We should neither be afraid of nor ignore the devil, because the moment we became born-again, we were already engaged in a spiritual battle against him. The key to victory is your ability to recognize the enemy and use the weapons God has given you to use against him.

What are those weapons? Faith is a weapon. Praise is a weapon. The Word of God is our sword! The truth is a weapon against the enemy, and it dismantles the lies of the kingdom of darkness. Every time we pray, read the Word, or confess God's Word, we are affecting the kingdom of darkness. There is no need to fear! The blood of the Lamb covers you. The Bible tells us that we wrestle against principalities and powers whose preferred battleground is the mind of the believer. Years ago, I discovered that the authority that I possessed was stronger than anything in the kingdom of darkness, and the same is true of you. Stand up, and put your armor on! Oh, and by the way, I already know the ending: you win!

Day 81: Power Prayer

Father, in the name of Jesus Christ, I thank You for who You are and all that You have done. You said in Your Word that the weapons of our warfare are not carnal, but mighty through God, to the pulling down of strongholds: casting down imaginations, and every high thing that exalts itself against the knowledge of God. (See 2 Corinthians 10:4–5.) I declare that the weapons I possess are stronger than the weapons of my enemy. You said in Your Word that You have given us power to tread on serpents and scorpions, over all the power of the enemy, and that nothing shall by any means hurt us (see Luke 10:19); therefore, I declare that nothing the enemy can throw my way has the power to hurt me or affect me, in the name of Jesus. I take authority over all the powers of darkness, and bring them under subjection to the name and authority of Jesus Christ. I declare that greater is He who lives in me than he who lives in the world. I serve the powers of darkness notice today that I will not be afraid nor will I back down from any of their vicious assaults against me or my family. I declare that I am strong in the Lord and in the power of His might. No weapon fashioned against me will prosper in the name of Jesus. I cast down all imaginations, thoughts, or suggestions that are designed to intimidate or produce fear in my life. I stand victorious against the enemy because Jesus has already defeated him on the cross and made a public spectacle of him before the entire universe. I declare that I win every spiritual battle in the name of Jesus. Amen!

Day 82: Piercing the Darkness

For God, who commanded the light to shine out of darkness, hath shined in our hearts, to give the light of the knowledge of the glory of God in the face of Jesus Christ.

(2 Corinthians 4:6)

One of the recurring themes of prophetic ministry is the correlation between light and darkness. Light is the antithesis of darkness, which means that we can never dwell in both at the same time. A part of our prophetic DNA is the ability and desire to expose darkness. Why? Because the light of Christ resides in us. Whether you realize it or not, the light in you (as a born-again believer) always exasperates the darkness around you. Have you ever wondered why there are certain people who dislike you or fight against you for no apparent reason? It has nothing to do with your personality; it has to do with the fact that the light in you agitates them! Often, they don't even recognize what is taking place.

One day, a coworker came to me and said, "I don't like you!" I asked why, and their response was, "I just don't like you." It is not personal! Rather, it is simply a principle: light can never get along with darkness. Before we were born again, darkness filled our hearts; but God, working in us, brought us His light: *"For God, who commanded the light to shine out of darkness, hath shined in our hearts."* The word *"shine"* there is the Greek word *lampō*, which means "to radiate brilliance." When we accepted the truth of the gospel, it caused the light of God's Word to radiate in our heart. Now our hearts are no longer overwhelmed by darkness because the light of truth has pierced through the black that once ruled. Now we must allow that same light to pierce through the darkness in the people we love and care about.

Day 82: Power Prayer

Father, in the name of Jesus Christ, I thank You for who You are and all that You have done in my life. I declare that Your light shines in my heart. The light of the gospel of Jesus Christ pierced through every form of darkness that lived within me. I declare that this brilliant light shines in and through me, and touches everyone around me. I recognize that light is superior to darkness; therefore, I declare that the darkness around me must scatter. I declare that any spiritual darkness, ignorance, or blindness operating in my loved ones is dissipated right now by the power of the Word of God. I declare that the love of God permeates my heart, and causes me to see things from God's perspective. I declare that I no longer walk in darkness, but I dwell in Your eternal light. I declare that there is no darkness in me. I will never stumble, fall, nor be confused, because the brilliance of Your presence is made manifest in my life. Thank You for sending Your light upon my loved ones. I declare that they, too, will receive the light of Your Word, and be transformed by the power of Your love in the name of Jesus. Amen!

232

Day 83: The Children's Bread

But Jesus said unto her, Let the children first be filled: for it is not meet to take the children's bread, and to cast it unto the dogs. (Mark 7:27)

What does it really mean to be a child of Abraham? We see this expression several times in the New Testament, but what does it really mean? I believe that most Christians are not experiencing the full manifestation of their spiritual heritage in Christ. Jesus revealed the spiritual inheritance to one woman in the gospel of Mark. She was a Syro-Phoenician, an ethnic group then despised by the Jews. This woman boldly approached Jesus and asked Him if He could heal her daughter. To this Jesus replied that it is not fitting to give the children's bread to dogs. Many Christians probably would've converted to another religion at this point! Yet this woman persisted in her faith, and ultimately received the miracle that she was searching for. This is an amazing story of faith and courage.

However, there is another dynamic to the story that we often overlook. Jesus referred to something called the *"children's bread."* What's that? The children's bread was an idiomatic expression that referred to the promises and blessings given to the children of Abraham. In other words, as children of Abraham, the Jewish people were entitled to healing, deliverance, breakthrough, and prosperity. In Christ, you and I are entitled to the same thing—and even greater! In essence, healing is not just something God *might* do for us if it is His will, but healing is, rather, the birthright of every believer. The same is true of any other promise in the Word of God. If healing, deliverance, and prosperity are the children's bread, then why are so many of God's people living beneath their birthright? I believe that many Christians don't realize that they are in fact the children of Abraham, and therefore joint heirs of the promise. Beloved, stop behaving like a Syro-Phoenician. Stop settling for scraps. Thanks to the work Christ did on the cross, it is now time for you to eat at the Master's table.

Day 83: Power Prayer

Father, in the name of Jesus Christ, I thank You for Your goodness and grace toward me. I declare that I am a seed of Abraham and therefore that I am entitled to the children's bread. I receive my healing, deliverance, breakthrough, peace, and prosperity in the name of Jesus Christ. I declare that I will no longer settle for scraps or crumbs, but I will eat at the Father's table. I will never allow the enemy to talk me out of my birthright again. I declare that I am blessed, healed, delivered, and made whole by the blood of Jesus Christ. I walk in the fullness of God because I am an heir of God, and a joint heir with Jesus Christ. I am a part of God's royal family. I will never behave, think, or perceive like a pauper, because I am a king and a priest unto God through the blood of Jesus Christ. Thank You, Lord, for Your faithfulness in my life. I thank You that my family members are consecrated to You through my profession of faith in the name of Jesus. I sanctify my children, family, loved ones, coworkers, and neighbors to Your divine purpose for their lives. I walk in the blessing of Abraham all the days of my life in the name of Jesus. Amen!

Day 84: The Law of Confession

*That if thou shalt confess with thy mouth the Lord Jesus,
and shalt believe in thine heart that God hath raised him
from the dead, thou shalt be saved.* (Romans 10:9)

What you say is what you get! Often, I hear Christians dismissively say, "Oh that's just that name it and claim it stuff!" Even though I agree that there has been much abuse of this truth, I want to show you that it is absolutely biblical to say that faith is the key to manifesting kingdom living. Without the right knowledge of faith, we will never be able to walk in victory. In the natural world there are natural laws; the same is true of the spiritual realm. There are spiritual laws that govern the kingdom of God.

One of the most important spiritual laws that exist in the kingdom of God is the law of confession. What do I mean by the law of confession? Well, the Bible tells us in Romans 10 that if we confess with the mouth that Jesus is Lord, and believe in our heart that God has raised Him from the dead, we shall be saved. The Greek word for confession here is the word *homologeo* which means "to say the same thing as another." Essentially, to confess means to say what God says. The more we learn to *say* what God says, and *believe* what God says, the more we will *have* what God says.

As simple as this principle seems, many people violate it. In other words, they say the opposite of what God says and still expect to see blessings in their life. Beloved, nothing could be further from the truth. Until you are aligning your *mouth* with heaven, you will not be able to align your *life* with heaven. Remember, right thinking leads to right speaking, which leads to right believing, and ultimately produces right living. Jesus put it this way, *"Whatever things you ask when you pray, believe that you receive them, and you will have them"* (Mark 11:24 NKJV). What would happen if you really believed that you would have everything you said? You would probably change what you're saying! Well, guess what? You *will* have whatever you say!

Day 84: Power Prayer

Father, in the name of Jesus Christ, I thank You for who You are and all that You have done in my life. I know that Your Word is the final authority concerning matters in heaven and in earth. Your Word says that I will have whatever I say, therefore, I only speak Your Words. I declare that my mouth is filled with the Word of God, and I will only say what Your Word says. I will not contradict Your Word with negative confessions, thoughts, or speech; instead, I will align my mouth with heaven's divine agenda. I recognize that my words have power; therefore, I choose to speak life and not death. I declare that life and death is in the power of my tongue, therefore, I release the blessing of the Lord over my life and the life of my loved ones. I declare that I am healed, I declare that I am blessed, and I declare that I am prosperous in the name of Jesus. I choose to use my mouth as a weapon to destroy the enemy's kingdom, and as a tool to build the kingdom of God. I refuse to curse my enemies; instead, I choose to bless them. I declare that the power of God is working for me and through me to accomplish God's perfect will in my life in the name of Jesus. Amen!

Day 85: Speak to My Heart

Again, he limiteth a certain day, saying in David, To day, after so long a time; as it is said, To day if ye will hear his voice, harden not your hearts. (Hebrews 4:7)

Sometime ago, I went through a season in my life when I found it extremely difficult to hear God's voice. Every time I prayed, it was difficult to feel God's presence. I found myself growing almost apathetic toward ministry. As you can imagine, this was very frustrating and discouraging. I began to cry out to God and ask Him to speak to me. One of the Scriptures that resonated with me during this time was Hebrews 4:7. In this particular verse, the writer of Hebrews admonishes us to not harden our hearts. (Many Christians don't realize how hard their hearts can become!)

As I began to daily pray this prayer found in Hebrews, something began to happen on the inside of me. It culminated one day when I felt the presence of an angel behind me. I turned around and saw a tall angel standing there with a bucket of water in his hand. He lifted it high and poured this crystal spring water on top of me. The water was so cold that when it hit my body, I jumped up in the air and begin to speak in tongues. I began to sing praises unto God like never before, and my heart was filled with excitement. I asked the angel his name, and he responded, "My name is Joy." My heart no longer felt heavy or cold anymore. I had experienced a beautiful supernatural awakening within my heart that was God's direct answer to my prayer that my heart would not be hardened.

We must be careful not to allow our hearts to become hardened. The Holy Spirit desires to speak to us in a very intimate way, but we must make provision for this to take place. We make provision for the Holy Spirit by monitoring the condition of our hearts. What area do you need the Lord to speak to you in? What is it that you need to hear from God? The Holy Spirit is speaking right now! All we need to do is remove the dross from our hearts so that we can hear His voice. Do not allow situations and circumstances to harden your heart. If you have not been able to hear from God lately, simply beseech Him daily to speak to your heart. Ask Him to purify your heart. The moment He does, you will be amazed by what you hear!

Day 85: Power Prayer

Father, in the name of Jesus Christ, I thank You for Your amazing love toward me. I declare that my heart is open to hearing Your voice. I ask You to remove anything from my heart that is blocking my ability to hear Your voice. Holy Spirit, speak to me now. I declare that my heart is a divine reservoir for Your Word. I declare that my heart is receptive to divine wisdom, knowledge, and understanding. My heart is the supernatural repository of Your love, Your truth, and Your wisdom. I thank You, Lord, for directing my path and ordering my steps according to Your Word. I look to You for my strength and security, and I thank You for being the Lord of my life. You said in Your Word that Your sheep hear Your voice and they will not follow the voice of a stranger. I declare that I am Your sheep, and I hear Your voice. I will not follow the voice of a stranger. I declare that Your Spirit leads and guides me at all times and in every situation. Today, I declare that I am a hearer and a doer of Your Word in the name of Jesus, amen!

Day 86: No Turning Back

And Jesus said unto him, No man, having put his hand to the plough, and looking back, is fit for the kingdom of God. (Luke 9:62)

Every summer, I used to attend a Christian camp (in fact, it was at this camp that I met the most beautiful woman I had ever seen—who later somehow agreed to become my wife!). One of the best activities at the camp was a huge zip line high up in the mountains. To reach it, you climbed straight up for what seem like forever. Once you reached a certain point in the climb, you actually didn't have a chance to turn around again. The camp worker would remind us, "the only way down the mountain is the zip line!"

This reminds me of our spiritual lives. Jesus told us that if we place our hands upon the plow, and look back, we are not fit for the kingdom. In other words, we have to make a decision and stick with it. There's only one way down the mountain! Many times, the enemy of our soul will attempt to talk us out of the blessings and promises of God for our lives. For example, maybe you have been believing God for healing in your body, but it seems like nothing has happened. Don't listen to the enemy telling you to look back, to regret your prayers, to think, *Maybe I should stop praying and go back down the mountain—nothing's happening!* Do not allow the enemy to talk you down from your spiritual zip line. Go all the way with God! Don't turn back! You are closer to your breakthrough than you realize.

Too many people are quitting prematurely. Right when they are about to experience a miracle in their life, they give up. Beloved, don't be among those who turn around. Make a decision that God's Word is the final authority and that you will believe it no matter what, and then stick with that decision.

Day 86: Power Prayer

Father, in the name of Jesus Christ, I thank You for who You are and all that You have done in my life. I declare that Your Word is the final authority in my life, and I refuse to turn back. I declare that You are the Source of my strength and my life, and I will not fear anything the enemy throws at me. I declare that I am consistent, I am vigilant, I am persistent in the things of God. I will never look back! Your Word is true and is a sure foundation upon which I stand. I put my hand to the kingdom plow, and I commit myself to my relationship with You. I will not vacillate nor turn around. I will not waver nor be double-minded in the name of Jesus. Lord, I ask You for strength in the areas in which I am weak. I refuse to succumb to the pressure of the enemy. I know that greater is the One who lives in me than he that is in the world. I declare that it is well with me and with my entire house in the name of Jesus. Amen!

243

Day 87: Strength in the Inner Man

That he would grant you, according to the riches of his glo-ry, to be strengthened with might by his Spirit in the inner man. (Ephesians 3:16)

In the United States, food is a multibillion dollar industry. We spend more money eating out per capita than any other nation in the world. In fact, I was shocked—and pleasantly surprised—when I traveled overseas and noticed how small restaurant portions are in other countries compared to America. I don't mean to pick on the US; people in every nation focus a lot of energy on food, and a lot of energy on their physical appearance. However, no matter what country you're in, one of the most neglected aspects of the human experience is the inner man. As Christians, we must recognize that there is much more to our existence than our physical bodies! We must recognize that we are spirits, who possess souls, and live in a human bodies.

When God created Adam in the garden of Eden, He breathed into his nostrils the breath of life and Adam became a living being. (See Genesis 2:7.) Notice that Adam was just dirt until God breathed His Spirit into him! The same is true of us; without a spirit living on the inside of us, we are nothing more than dust. The Bible affirms this truth in Ephesians 3, where Paul prays a very powerful prayer over the Ephesian church. He prays that they would be strengthened with might by the Holy

Spirit in their inner being. I believe that this is God's will for us today, that we would be strengthened with might by the Holy Spirit in our inward man. Our spirit is more powerful than our physical body; therefore, when our spirit is strong, every other area of our life is strengthened. Maybe you have felt weak spiritually; well, God wants to strengthen you today. He desires to empower you in your inner being. Your spirit is the part of you that has direct contact with God. Without a strong spirit man, you will not be able to live a strong spiritual life. However, when your spirit is strengthened, you will be able to manifest the supernatural in every area of your life.

245

Day 87: Power Prayer

Father, in the name of Jesus Christ, I thank You for Your power and might working in my inner being. I declare that I am strong in You and in the power of Your might. I declare that I am spiritually alert and aware of Your presence. I refuse to succumb to the distractions of the enemy in my life. I know that it is Your will for me to always flourish in my spirit, soul, and body. Your Word declares that my eye has not seen, nor my ears heard, neither has entered into my heart the things which You have prepared for those who love you (see 1 Corinthians 2:9), but You have revealed them to me by Your Spirit. I thank You for the revelation of the Holy Spirit in my inner being, which is producing in me a desire to do what is pleasing in Your sight. I declare the work of the Holy Spirit is made manifest in every area of my spiritual life. I thank You for Your miraculous power in my spirit, soul, and body in the name of Jesus. Amen!

Day 88: Rivers of Living Water

In the last day, that great day of the feast, Jesus stood and cried, saying, If any man thirst, let him come unto me, and drink. He that believeth on me, as the scripture hath said, out of his belly shall flow rivers of living water. (But this spake he of the Spirit, which they that believe on him should receive: for the Holy Ghost was not yet given; because that Jesus was not yet glorified.) (John 7:37–39)

Prophecy is the nature and characteristic of everyone who believes in Jesus. But what is the source of the prophetic? What gives us the confidence to open our mouths and prophesy to a situation, knowing that it must respond to what we say? Jesus calls to all who are listening and to us today, and He says "Come to Me and drink. And anyone who believes in Me will have rivers of living water flow out of his belly." The belly He is referring to here is the Spirit of God residing inside the spirit of the one who believes in Jesus. The Holy Spirit is the One who enables us to prophesy.

But when Jesus made this invitation, the Holy Spirit had not yet been released to the believers. Jesus was advertising the soon-coming glory that the early church would walk in after He was resurrected and ascended to the Father. In the book of Acts, as the early church was gathered on the day of Pentecost, they were all filled with the Holy Spirit and began to speak in other languages. This was a supernatural work of the Holy Spirit.

To each other they probably sounded like they babbled, but to the Jews who were worshipping at the time in Jerusalem, they were declaring the wonders of God. When the apostle Peter responded to this supernatural occurrence, he declared that this was the fulfillment of the word of the prophet Joel: *"...in the last days, saith God, I will pour out of my Spirit upon all flesh: and your sons and your daughters shall prophesy,..."* (Acts 2:17). The early church received an impartation from God to prophesy when the Holy Spirit was given. In an instant, they were transformed from just "the early church" to the "prophesying church."

The promise Jesus had made in John 7 was now fulfilled. Now, through the Holy Spirit released, you and I and every believer, when praying, can not only petition God but can also be supernaturally enabled to proclaim the mind of God and release rivers of living water from their innermost being. Everything the early church walked in is yours. Open your mouth and prophesy!

248

Day 88: Power Prayer

Father, I thank You for who You are and all that You have done. Father, I ask that You fill me up with Your Holy Spirit, and I thank You that Your Word declares that if I believe in You, rivers of living water will begin to flow out of my innermost being. (Place your hand on your stomach and say,) I release the river of living water to flow out of me right now in the name of Jesus. I thank You, Lord, for pouring out of Your Spirit upon me. I have now been supernaturally empowered to bring about transformation and change every time I pray. I will not be silent, but I will open my mouth to prophesy and declare the Word of God over every situation in my life and see it change in the name of Jesus Christ.

249

Day 89: Overcoming Hopelessness

Therefore if any man be in Christ, he is a new creature: old things are passed away; behold, all things are become new.
(2 Corinthians 5:17)

Before we became born again, we were helpless victims of our situation, bound to a defeated path predetermined for us by the actions of our parents and all who came before us. It's similar to the genetic characteristics that we inherit from our parents. When you walk into a hospital waiting room, before you can be seen by a doctor, the first thing you have to do is fill out a medical history form because it has been discovered that some people are genetically predisposed to certain diseases. We look to our parents to guesstimate whether we'll go bald, how poor our eyesight will become—and even what our life expectancy is!

But perhaps this physical reality has over-influenced our spiritual perception. We tend to surrender too easily to faults that we have always struggled with or that we think are inevitable, thanks to our family genes. However, the Scripture clearly states that if you are in Christ, *you are a new creature!* The old has passed away and the new has come; therefore all things are become new. Simply put, when we become born again believers, we are now in Jesus Christ and everything has changed. Your old reality has been done away with. Although you may still look the same on the outside, there is something completely brand new at work on the inside of you. You now possess the DNA of the new man. Your old genes have been erased and you have now been configured with the new nature. What will your new nature look like?

Day 89: Power Prayer

Father, in the name of Jesus, Your Word declares that if any man be in Christ, he is a new creature and old things are passed away; therefore, I declare that I am a new creation in Christ. I declare that I walk in the newness of life. I declare that every old, dilapidated, outdated, and dead thing in my life has been removed and the new has come into manifestation. I will never be bound by hopelessness, depression, fear, or despair again. Just like a newborn baby is fresh and brand new, I declare that I am fresh and pure in Christ. I cast down every lie of the evil one which suggests that I am just the same as I ever was. The devil is a liar! I reject every thought, idea, or suggestion that would attempt to keep me in the past in my thinking or behavior in the name of Jesus. I am born from above. I am new species of being—a Christ-like species. I declare that my life is full of Your love and power in the name of Jesus. Amen!

251

Day 90: Be of Good Courage

Be strong and of a good courage, fear not, nor be afraid of them: for the LORD thy God, he it is that doth go with thee; he will not fail thee, nor forsake thee. (Deuteronomy 31:6)

My father was a military man, and so, as you can imagine, I have had my fair share of pep talks on courage. In my family, we were simply not allowed to back down from a fight or confrontation. Once, when I was being bullied by a big kid at school, my father told me I couldn't come home unless I confronted this bully! I doubt that would be a popular parenting solution today, but back then it was common to experience such tough love. And although that particular scenario did not turn out with me on top, I did learn a very valuable lesson by not backing down from this bully: I learned the value of courage.

Courage is not the absence of fear; rather, courage is the ability and the boldness to do what is required of you even when fear is present. The word *"courage"* actually means "boldness or bravery." God told the Israelites to be of good courage. They were probably thinking, *How can we be courageous? We're one of the smallest nations around, and some of these other nations hate us!* Well, the reason they could be courageous is because God was with them. I want you to know today that God is with you. You don't have to cave in to fear, because the One who watches over you is greater than anything or anyone who can come against you. Simply put, if God is for you, who can be against you?

One thing I have learned about the Lord is that He will always come through for us, no matter what. It does not matter what the situation looks like on the outside, know in your heart that God will never leave you nor forsake you. I don't know how that makes you feel, but it makes me want to give God a big shout of praise! The kingdom of God is not for pansies. During World War II, the Soviet Union would actually shoot their own soldiers if they ever defected or ran from battle. Thankfully, we don't serve an evil dictator like the Soviets did, but the God we serve still requires courage from us. We have to make a decision to trust God in every situation of our lives (which should be far easier than placing our trust in any earthly leader or general!). The moment we make this decision, I believe that the spirit of courage will come upon us. Do not be afraid or dismayed, beloved, because God is with you, and He will deliver you from any and every peril in your life. Be of good courage!

253

Day 90: Power Prayer

Father, in the name of Jesus Christ, I thank You for Your great love toward me. I declare that You are the God who fights every battle in my life. I declare that I do not need to be afraid of what the enemy will bring against me in the name of Jesus. I declare that I am courageous and bold in You because I recognize that if You are for me, no one can be against me. I fight on Your side, because I recognize that You are the winning side. I declare that great boldness and courage flourish on the inside of me right now. I declare that I am surrounded by an entire host of angelic armies at my beck and call who are ready to defend me. You give your angels charge over me to keep me in all of my ways. I declare that I will never be overtaken by fear, anxiety, worry, or terror in the name of Jesus. I declare that I will take the power of these 90 days with me into the future, to serve You fearlessly. I declare that I am full of faith and courage in the name of Jesus, amen!

About the Author

Pastor Kynan T. Bridges is the senior pastor of Grace & Peace Global Fellowship in Tampa, Florida. Through his profound revelation of the Word of God and his dynamic teaching ministry, Pastor Bridges has revolutionized the lives of many in the body of Christ. Through his practical approach to applying the deep truths of the Word of God, he reveals the authority and identity of the new covenant believer.

God has placed on Pastor Kynan a peculiar anointing for understanding and teaching the Scriptures, along with the gift of prophecy and healing. Pastor Kynan and his wife, Gloria, through an apostolic anointing, are committed to equipping the body of Christ to live in the supernatural every day and to fulfill the Great Commission. It is the desire of Pastor Kynan to see the nations transformed by the unconditional love of God.

A highly sought speaker and published author of several books including *Kingdom Authority* (Whitaker House, 2015) and *Power of Prophetic Prayer* (Whitaker House, 2016), Pastor Kynan is also a committed husband, a mentor, and a father to his four beautiful children: Ella, Naomi, Isaac, and Israel.